THE PAS D
NORTH-W

Arthur Eperon is one of the most experi..
travel writers in Europe. Since leaving the RAF in 1945 he h..
worked as a journalist in various capacities, often involving travel.
He has concentrated on travel writing for the past twenty-five
years and contributed to many publications including *The Times*,
Daily Telegraph, *New York Times*, *Woman's Own*, *Popular Motoring*
and the *TV Times*. He has also appeared on radio and television
and for five years was closely involved in Thames Television's
programme *Wish You Were Here*. He has been wine writer to the
RAC publications and a number of magazines.

He has an intimate and extensive knowledge of France and its
food and wine as a result of innumerable visits there over the last
forty years. In 1974 he won the *Prix des Provinces de France*, the
annual French award for travel writing. His *Travellers' France*
topped the paperback bestseller list for eleven weeks.

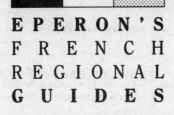

EPERON'S FRENCH REGIONAL GUIDES

PAS DE CALAIS & NORTH-WEST FRANCE

ARTHUR EPERON

PAN BOOKS
LONDON, SYDNEY AND AUCKLAND

First published 1991 by Pan Books Ltd
Cavaye Place, London SW10 9PG

1 3 5 7 9 8 6 4 2

© Arthur Eperon 1991
Illustrations © Mary Fraser 1991
Maps © Ken Smith 1991

The right of Arthur Eperon to be identified as author of this
work has been asserted by him in accordance with the Copyright
Designs and Patents Act 1988.

ISBN 0 330 31737 7

Designed by Peter Ward
Photoset by Parker Typesetting Service Leicester
Printed in England by Clays Ltd, St Ives plc

CONTENTS

1   *Departments of France*

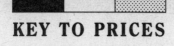

KEY TO PRICES

ROOMS		MEALS	
A = Under 100F		A = Under 75F	
B = 100–150F		B = 75–90F	
C = 150–200F		C = 90–125F	
D = 200–250F		D = 125–150F	
E = 250–350F		E = 150–175F	
F = 350–450F		F = 175–225F	
G = over 450F		G = over 225F	

Room prices per night for double room without breakfast.
Meal prices include tax and service.

INTRODUCTION

The north-west of France is unknown country. Except in wars, Picardie, Artois, Flanders and Pas de Calais have been almost neglected by the rest of France, culturally and economically. Parisians rarely think of visiting any of these areas except on business or when passing through to cross the Channel. Even the millions of Britons who land at the Channel ports stop off only briefly to take on supplies before hurrying to the motorways to make for their holiday *gîtes* or hotels in the Loire, Dordogne, or on the Aquitaine or Mediterranean coasts. Only recently have a few Britons discovered the charming treasures which lie a few miles inland – wood-covered hillsides, farming hamlets alongside trout streams, secluded narrow lanes, and lush valleys of little-known rivers like the Course, the Canche, the Aa and the Lys. There are some wonderful places to hide away and some splendid places to stay and to eat. The region has charming village inns, manor houses converted into small hotels, and beautifully furnished old châteaux where you feel like a family friend rather than a hotel guest.

All this is within a few minutes' drive of the great Channel ports, bases from which for centuries would-be conquerors tried to invade England and which are now invaded daily by thousands of English tourists.

Nine million people travel through Calais port each year. Three million use Boulogne, which is also the biggest fresh-fish port in the EC. Dunkerque's ferry traffic is growing though it remains a freight port for container ships and oil tankers. Despite all this port activity and the importance of industrial towns like Lille, Abbeville and Amiens, and despite motorways reaching Dunkerque and creeping very close to Calais and Boulogne, the north-west remains a quiet, almost hidden country where a man is measured by the number and health of his cows and not the cost of his car, and the church is the centre of the village. Its

Cap Blanc Nez

culture, its food, its villages, its atmosphere are more Flemish than French. You can see this especially in the local fêtes and festivals which are really joyous occasions. The Dunkerque Mardi Gras celebrations are surpassed only by the Ostend Festival over the Belgian border.

Stretches of countryside are flat and rather melancholy, scarred still by battles and by the remains of dated industries and played-out mines, but you can avoid these by taking little local roads.

First we will follow the coast beginning just south of the Somme river estuary, where the Somme department meets Normandy.

Somme is one of the three modern departments which used to be called Picardie. The others are Oise and Aisne. The Somme coastline is very short, and the first little resort across the river Bresle which divides Somme from Normandy, Les Mers-les-Bains, is really a suburb of the Normandy resort of Le Tréport. But the famous Tréport cliffs soon give way to the estuary and to the sandbanks in the Baie de Somme.

North of the bay is a coastal plain, La Marquenterre, which has built up between the Somme and Authie river estuaries since the Middle Ages, when the town of Rue was a coastal port. Debris of soil and stone was washed against the coast by currents, and formed coastal flats of sand and mud. The flats are now protected as a bird sanctuary and there is one little beach resort here – Fort-Mahon-Plage. Across the Authie, on a coast of sands, is a series of little beach resorts between Berck-Plage, which is a treatment centre for bone illnesses, and Le Touquet Paris-Plage, still one of the smart resorts of northern France, if not quite so fashionable as when stars such as Noël Coward and multimillionaires had weekend homes there.

Beaches and sand dunes continue to the edge of Boulogne, the ferry and fishing port. Then hills and cliffs rise to the tall, grey cliffs of Cap Gris Nez, for which cross-Channel swimmers aim, and on to Cap Blanc Nez where the cliffs begin to slope down to Calais. Past Calais the sand dunes continue to the industrial port of Dunkerque and on to Dunkerque beaches and the Belgian border. This is true old Flanders where people eat heartily, work and play hard, and where the influence of the old Flemish tongue is obvious in the place names.

The flat country inland from Dunkerque is criss-crossed with the old canals of Flanders. They continue down to St Omer, the old town around which are grown some of the best vegetables in France, then go westward to Calais and deviate to Gravelines, which is on the coast between Dunkerque and Calais. This is not beautiful country, but there are some charming and interesting little old towns, such as Bergues, inland from Dunkerque, Cassel towards St Omer, historic Guines, and likeable Ardres behind Calais.

The A25 motorway from Dunkerque runs parallel to the Belgian border to the big industrial city of Lille, a great place to eat. From here the A1 motorway continues to Paris and connecting motorways take you to Brussels, into Germany and right through to Munich.

Lille is the centre of the old mining and industrial area around Béthune, Lens, Douai and Cambrai – names known as bloody battlefields of the First World War. Arras is the one town which still has true charm for travellers.

The great beauty of north-west France is also found inland between Boulogne and Calais, and around the beautiful medieval hilltop town of Montreuil. It is in these areas that the British have been seeking their cottages and houses to live in with 'one foot in France', and by doing this they have forced up the price of everything from bourgeois villas to half-abandoned *fermettes*.

Here you can find woodlands like the thick Boulogne Forest, with lovely walks and quiet picnic spots, the hilly Guines Forest, and the Hardelot Forest, behind a beach resort beloved by families and golfers. You can get lost in a maze of lovely narrow lanes, suddenly finding a gem of a farmyard unchanged for fifty years; a true village church with a cemetery of ornate, proud tombs; a simple auberge where the first menu costs fifty francs and nearly all the customers are locals; or come upon a hidden little bridge over a stream and find that it leads to a village square. I feel sorry for people so harried and full of care that they must drive on the abominable N1 and breathe its killer fumes.

Pas de Calais is a land for following little rivers. For years we took a charming route from Boulogne to Montreuil, whether we were heading for the Pyrenees or mooching around Montreuil and Le Touquet. We turned right off the N42 to drive through the Boulogne Forest to Crémarest, and took another forest road through Desvres Forest to pick up the D127 which negotiates the old pottery town of Desvres to run along the delightful valley of the river Course to Montreuil.

The same D127 runs alongside an arm of the Calais canal from Calais to Guines and then offers a delightful route through the Guines Forest and the villages of Parc Régional to Desvres. You can follow it all the way from Calais to Montreuil and almost every kilometre passes interesting or attractive scenery.

From Montreuil, the N39 to Étaples runs alongside the river Canche, but you cannot see it, so it is better to follow the white roads south of the river marked on your yellow Michelin map.

From Montreuil to the historic little town of Hesdin, both sides of the Canche have attractive stretches, but the N39 can carry a lot of heavy trucks on weekdays, so the slower D113 is more fun.

To the south, on the borders of Somme and Pas de Calais departments, the Authie valley has a string of pleasant *'villages fleuris'* – an official title given to villages which make a special display of flowers on roadsides and in gardens. There are still many little undiscovered places to hide away in these valleys not far from the coast.

Crécy Forest in Somme has a very pretty road through it. Least known perhaps to the people belting down the N1 is the valley of the river Aa. Few people seem to have heard of it. From Lumbres, where the converted water-mill has become one of our favourite hotels, the river wanders fairly aimlessly through the countryside east and south of Desvres to meet the river Course very close to a trout farm. It passes through many quiet, unassuming farming hamlets and a few more lively villages, such as Fauquembergues and Hucqueliers.

Compiègne Forest, an oak and beech forest dating back to Charlemagne, and a favourite hunting ground of the French kings through centuries, is only 68km from Paris. It forms the southern section of a series of forest areas which are a delight to walkers, cyclists and unhurried motorists. There are beautiful little roads, forest tracks through firebreaks and marked footpaths with occasional hamlets and old hunting lodges, some of which have been turned into cafés or inns, where knowledgeable Parisians hide on weekends. Compiègne Forest runs into the d'Laigue and Ourscamps Carlepont Forests. They are all in the department of Oise, which Parisians would love to see swallowed up in their beloved Île de France; but it is part of old Picardie and belongs there with Somme and Aisne.

A few kilometres eastward in Aisne is Basse Forêt de Coucy, which merges into the delightful St Gobain Forest and almost reaches Laon, the superb hilltop city which was the seat of the French monarchs when Paris was a village.

Now that the A1 Lille-Paris and A26 motorways accommodate the heavy industrial traffic and the car-drivers hurrying from Belgium and Germany, the pleasant roads, forests and villages north of Paris are left free for people like me to explore.

Most Britons go south of Paris to see Fontainebleau, or belt down the motorway and drive round Paris on the bewildering and desperately crowded *périphérique*, then on to the motorway to the south. In *The Complete Travellers' France* (Pan, £5.99) I routed my readers through Compiègne and Gobain Forests to Laon and had effusively grateful letters from travellers who had never thought of going to these delightful spots before. This is a splendid way, too, through Champagne to Burgundy, the Rhône and Provence.

Because of the A1 motorway, parts of Picardie – and Oise in particular – have come to be regarded by some people as extensions of Paris. They are not. Delightful towns like Senlis, Beauvais and Chantilly maintain their own traditions, atmosphere and culture.

If the opening of the Channel Tunnel brings changes in the north, they are likely to come from a spread of industry westward from Lille towards St Omer and near the A26 motorway, which already runs near to Calais, and perhaps from across the Belgian border to the same area. South from Guines down to Montreuil, where you find the nicest countryside and villages, factories are very unlikely to replace the farms. There *has* been an invasion of Britons buying houses. They will not stay for ever. It took the French only 200 years to get the English out of Calais. And if Henry VIII did have his military headquarters at Guines, François I, the equally flamboyant womanizer, had his down the road at Ardres. They met in 1520 at the Field of the Cloth of Gold to make an alliance and swear eternal friendship between England and France. Like most summits, it was a disaster, but at least it was the best picnic the world has ever seen (*see* Guines, page 143).

Most of the little towns and villages of Pas de Calais have their own little historic tales to tell. Before the Second World War many English families ventured abroad each summer to the beaches at the little resorts of Wissant and Wimereux (which they called Wimeroo). I went back in the early 1950s to see what had become of these little pieces of paradise. In a small hotel in Wissant they told me proudly that General de Gaulle himself was married to the daughter of a former Mayor of Calais. 'When he comes on a visit,' they whispered, 'he stays here – incognito!'

which shows that you will have no problem about scandal, whoever you take with you to the Pas de Calais. People who could pretend that they had not recognized General de Gaulle must be of the very essence of discretion.

HOW TO GO

AIR
London Heathrow–Lille (Air France)
Lydd (Kent)–Le Touquet (British Independent Airways)

CAR FERRIES/HOVERCRAFT
Dover/Folkstone–Boulogne, Sealink, P & O (1 hr 40 mins)
Dover–Calais, Sealink, P & O (1 hr 15 mins–1 hr 40 mins)
Newhaven–Dieppe in Normandy, Sealink Dieppe Ferries (4 hrs)
Ramsgate–Dunkerque, Sally Line (2 hrs 30 mins)
Dover–Ostend in Belgium, P & O (3 hrs 30 mins)
Dover–Boulogne/Calais, Hoverspeed (35–40 mins)

At Boulogne fast trains run from the station alongside the hoverport (Boulogne-Aeroglisseurs) to Amiens and Paris.

FOOD

The great American foreign correspondent and connoisseur of European food, Waverley Root, showed all the prejudices of a Parisian bourgeois when he wrote about the food of what he called 'the Flatlands' in his book *The Food of France*:

'Dullness is the characteristic of this area. The blight extends even to food, probably less interesting here than in any other part of France.'

That is just a politer way of calling the cooking of Picardie and the north 'peasant', as polite society has done for generations. Meals in the north certainly are satisfying, full of flavour, owe more to the farmhouse kitchen than to the modern cookery schools, and owe far more to traditional cooking than to nouvelle cuisine, except where a young chef from the cookery schools has taken over a posh restaurant.

The ingredients of the north are absolutely superb and they are prepared and cooked to suit the active and quite hard life of the people and the climate. That is what I call good regional cooking.

I have always believed that the best fish comes from cold waters, that the North Sea and the Atlantic offer on the whole better fresh fish than the warmer and polluted Mediterranean. A third of all fish landed in France is landed in Boulogne. Most of the fish eaten in Paris comes from Boulogne. The boats unload the catches alongside stalls on the harbour's edge and the people of Pas de Calais like to see it 'leap straight into the pan' – cooked in butter, on the bone and served with a shellfish garnish or a simple fish *fumet* sauce with mushrooms and cream. The freshness matters more than the presentation on the plate. Sole is especially superb. Cod (*cabillaud*) is usually very good and so is ling (*lingue*). Boats do in fact bring in some Mediterranean fish and some from the coasts of Africa, including sardines, red mullet and rascasse, the ugly fish which I find almost inedible on its own but which is regarded as essential for bouillabaisse. Fish stews are popular under several names and a lot are very good. *Bouillabaisse du nord*, a fish soup-stew called *couquignoise*, made from mussels, leeks, onion and herbs, is very similar to the southern version. *Chaudrée à la boulognaise* is made of white cold-water fish with a lot of eel, garlic and white wine. It is named after the *chaudron* (cauldron) in which it is made.

One of the finest fish soups in France is made in Le Touquet by Serge Pérard, who sells it in his superb fish shop, his delightfully animated and good fish restaurant, and in bottles and containers which are sent all over the north of France, including Paris, where in many well-known restaurants it is served as a product of the house. I do admit to my guests where it comes from!

Although this is not wine country any more than Paris is, plenty is drunk and used for cooking. Boulogne's mussels are splendid and *moules à la marinière* (stewed in white wine with chopped shallot, parsley and bay leaf) is still the most popular way of serving them, though the Norman habit of adding cream

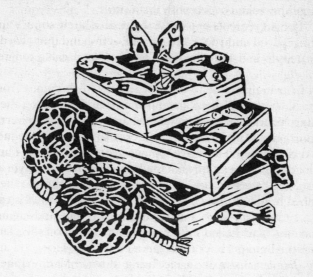

to the juice has spilled over the border. The lovely, tender, little mussels called *bouchots* after the posts on which they are cultivated are a speciality of Boulogne. Cockles are a speciality of the whole coast, and especially Dunkerque. They are called *henons* here, *coques* elsewhere.

Herrings and mackerel, salted, pickled or smoked, are part of family life in Flanders. Both fish are smoked in Dunkerque and Boulogne. They are called *bouffi* or *craquelot* and are rather like the old-style English bloater. The Mayor of Dunkerque throws them from the town hall balcony on the Sunday before Mardi Gras.

Harengs sour are salted and smoked herrings, sometimes called *gendarmes*. In Calais you might still find *hareng à la calaisienne* (herrings stuffed with roes, mushrooms, shallots and parsley, baked in paper cases). *Harengs de Bergues* or *haranguets* are smoked sprats (*esprots* in the rest of France), popular as snacks.

The famous Flemish *waterzooi* can be either a fish soup-stew or a chicken stew. The fish version is a *matelote* (stew of freshwater fish such as carp, perch and pike with herbs) to which vegetables and cream are added. The other is chicken stew with leeks and a sauce made with the stew stock and cream.

Jellied eels (*anguilles à la flamande*) are very popular, especially around Dunkerque. Traditionally they were cooked with herbs in beer to get rid of the fat. Now wine is often used.

Quenelles de brochet, little mousses made with pike, are sold fresh or in tins.

Nouvelle cuisine's slivers of carrot for décor never stood much chance in countryside where vegetables grow for mile upon mile, and some of the finest in Europe are grown in the market gardens around St Omer's waterways. They grow superb leeks, cauliflowers, sprouts (picked and served very young), carrots and chicory (which the French call *endive* or *chicorée*). Spinach and turnips are also delicious. Asparagus is excellent. *Asperges à la flamande* is asparagus served hot with melted butter and hot hard-boiled eggs cut in half. You mash your own egg into the butter. I have been served it for breakfast.

Jets de houblon are male-flower shoots of hop (which are no good for beer) boiled in salt water with a squeeze of lemon, usually served with poached eggs and fried bread. Sometimes cream is added.

It is a joy to be served superb cabbage with pride and not with apologies. Cabbage is shredded into stews. Red cabbage is a typical Flemish dish, stewed with vinegar, apples and sugar (*chou rouge à la flamande*), cooked in butter with onion and spices (*à la lilloise*) or stewed with bacon and apples (*à la valenciennes*).

Crème à la flamande is onion and potato soup – a very pleasant winter dish. The great traditional Flemish dish *hochepot* is still a delight to hard workers or families in winter. The name means stirpot or shakenpot. It is a soup-stew with many versions. A typical working family's *hochepot* is made with brisket of beef, bacon, other pork cuts (often pigs' ears), breast and shoulder of mutton or lamb, all stewed with mixed sliced vegetables of which cabbage and potatoes are almost essential; onions, leeks and carrots are rarely missing, and genièvre gin or juniper berries. The meat is browned in fat before stewing. The juice is often served first as soup, then meat and vegetables as a main course – like *pot-au-feu*; 'pepperpot' is an unusual mixture of mutton and pork with vegetables stewed in beer.

The north is beef and pork country, and beer is used extensively in cooking, not only because there is no wine made there and the beer is excellent, but also because beer takes most of the fattiness away from the meat. *Carbonade à la flamande* is the classic Flemish dish of beef and onions braised in herbs and beer. *Cachuse* is pork braised with onions. *Veau flamand* has an exotic touch, left over, perhaps, from the Spanish occupation, though it is claimed to have been brought back from the Holy Land by Crusaders. It is veal braised with dried apricots, prunes and raisins. Prunes and raisins are stewed with wild rabbit in *lapin valenciennes*.

Genièvre, gin heavily perfumed with juniper berries, which we usually call Dutch gin, is used in cooking quite often – even in *coq à la bière* (chicken cooked in beer and genièvre with mushrooms). Cooking in genièvre was one of the few Flemish touches stolen for nouvelle cuisine.

Plentiful and excellent pork produces some of the best charcuterie in France, and the meat factories of Lille send it tinned or in foil to many parts of the world, competing with the Belgian industry, but offering superior products. Splendid sausages are made, usually smoked. Arras produces famous *andouillettes* (chitterling sausages), mostly eaten hot. I do not like them. They were long regarded as a cheap dish for poorer families and were on really cheap menus. But many peasant dishes, like *cou d'oie farci* (stuffed goose neck), became gourmets' delights and modern gourmet guides, especially the 'nouvelle bible' Gault Millau guide, have adopted *andouillettes* as a gourmet dish. Black pudding (*boudin noir*) is made extensively in the north as it is almost anywhere in France, the Netherlands and Germany where pigs are plentiful.

Valenciennes specializes in lambs' tongues, either stuffed (*langues fourrées*) or smoked (*langues fumées* or *langues à la Lucullus* when served with *foie gras*).

Local pâtés of French Flanders are excellent and if you shop in a supermarket or cheaper charcuterie do make certain that you *are* buying these and not the lesser Belgian factory pâtés and terrines which are swamping chain supermarkets as they do in Britain.

The great pâté is *potje vleesch* (or flesh), a truly tasty terrine of veal, chicken and rabbit. Duck pâtés and *ballotines* made in restaurants or independent charcuteries are excellent in the north and in the Somme estuary. Amiens' gastronomic dish is a *pâté de caneton*. A duck is fried whole. Then it is surrounded by a forcemeat of duck and chicken livers, onion and herbs, wrapped in pastry and baked. It is served cold and sliced. The charcuteries in Amiens are famous and very tempting.

One of the simplest snacks or starters can be absolutely delicious if made well. Called *ficelle picarde*, it is very similar to *ficelle normande* – a salty pancake stuffed with mushrooms and ham in cream, sometimes with cheese, and heated in the oven.

Flamiche is delicious, too, if absolutely fresh – a leek, cheese and cream tart. Sometimes it is made with pumpkin but then is not so tasty.

A strange snack you can buy in charcuteries of Picardie and the north is *daussade* – a mixture of onions, lettuce and cream served in a chunk of baguette sliced down the centre. A similar snack is *pain daussé* – onions mashed in cider and served in bread.

Cakes and biscuits are satisfying rather than mouth-watering. Dunkerque's *kokeboterom* is a sweet brioche dotted with raisins. Lille is known for biscuits (*petits beurres*, and *gaufres* – a sort of waffle). *Macarons* (almond macaroons) are made at Douai, Amiens and Rouen, where they are called Duchesses de Rouen. *Mirlitons*, puff pastries with an almond cream filling, come from Rouen, but they appear in many areas with apple in them as well, including around Le Touquet. *Tuiles d'Amiens* are tasty chocolate and orange biscuits. Tarts of apples, prunes or pears are made all over Picardie and Pas de Calais, and an interesting conserve is *raisiné picard*, pear jam cooked in grape juice, eaten with a spoon. Apples baked in pastry-like dumplings are called *rabotes* in Picardie (*bourdelots* in Normandy).

Though cheeses of this whole north-west area are overshadowed by the splendid cheeses of Normandy, there are some well worth seeking. A tempting cheese to weight-watchers comes from Bergues, the medieval town near Dunkerque. Bergues cheese is very low in fat because it is washed with beer every day. Locals love to eat it with beer, too.

French versions of Dutch Gouda and Edam are made near

Lille – simply called Gouda or Edam Français. They have been made in the north since the French were cut off from the Netherlands by a treaty with England to keep out Louis XIV in 1670. Like the Dutch version, this French Gouda is eaten around Bordeaux with red wine – a tradition going back to the days when Bordeaux was part of English Aquitaine and traded heavily with the Netherlands and England. A longer-cured version of Edam is called Edam *etuvé*, with a stronger smell and flavour. Lille makes also *Mimolette*, very similar to Gouda, and reputedly the favourite cheese of Général de Gaulle. Farms and small dairies make *gris de Lille*, cured in beer and brine and known also as *gris puant* (stinky grey). An acquired taste, I am told. I have not yet acquired it. Another cheese is called *puant* when cured in beer and brine. That is the famous (or notorious) *Maroilles* from Aisne, named after the monastery of Maroilles where it was invented in the tenth century. Sometimes it smells and tastes as if it had been kept since then. A close relation to Maroilles comes from Laon (*baguette Laonnaise*) but I find that it tastes and smells of ammonia. *Boulette d'Avesnes* is made in Flemish farmhouses with buttermilk or in factories with *fromage blanc*, and contains herbs.

A good cheese if you can find it is *fromage hesdin*, also called *belval*, the monastery at which it is made. It is a mild cows' milk cheese, quite new, and praised by restaurant owners.

One of the greatest cheese shops in the world is in Boulogne, run by Philippe Olivier at 43 rue Thiers. He has three maturing cellars at different temperatures and humidities, and gets his cheeses (including Stilton) from farms, dairies and factories all over France and beyond. He has cheeses that connoisseurs have never tasted. To go round his cellars with him is not only a gastronomic education but also a great temptation to put on weight. In Paris, in London and all over France great restaurants boast 'Cheeses by Olivier'.

No wine is made in Picardie or Nord. They say that cider is the wine of the region. But beer is the local drink. Beer-drinking led to the variety and importance of charcuterie. The *brasseurs* (brewers) used the grain and dregs of their beer to feed pigs, and pork was made into charcuterie to nibble with the beer in brasseries. Most French bars except cocktail bars of hotels or posh restaurants now serve *pression* – draught beer, but I can remember when it was difficult to get except in workers' bars or brasseries. Bottled beer is mostly low fermentation lager-style, with higher carbonation than the British used to like. The invasion of these Continental beers in recent years has changed the habits of the young British, if not those of real-ale lovers and rugby players. There are some excellent strong beers from Pas de Calais and Flanders, even if not quite up to the strength and flavour of the great Belgian beers (especially the genuine head-blowing Belgian Trappiste made by monks).

St Leonard is a reasonably priced, flavoursome and good bottled beer from a little brewery in a village just outside Boulogne.

HISTORY

The stories of the Nord, of the Channel ports, and of Picardie have been so different through the centuries that it's hard to believe they're on the same continent.

In the twentieth century, almost every town and village has been cruelly battered or destroyed by foreign invaders. But there is little new about this. The flat lands have few natural defences, and throughout history invaders and foreign rulers made life hell for the inhabitants.

For centuries through the Middle Ages Flanders wavered between supporting France or England. The part of Flanders now in France was but a small bit of it. The Counts of Flanders' territory stretched from Dunkerque to the Ardennes, together with Belgian and Dutch Flanders. But after much fighting between Flanders and the King of France, Philip the Fair of France obtained Lille, Douai and Orchies by treaty in 1305. In other words, he acquired what centuries later became the rich industrial area of northern France. Then in the early fifteenth century Duke Philip of Burgundy married Margaret, the daughter of the Count of Flanders, who inherited Flanders in 1417. So the already powerful Duke of Burgundy, whose capital was Dijon, ruled also in Flanders, right to the sea. He moved his capital to Brussels and was a real threat to France. The country then got into a terrible tangle. The young King Charles VI was weak and sometimes became demented; John the Fearless, Duke of Burgundy, uncle of the King, and the King's rake of a brother, Louis of Orleans, fought for power in France. Among Louis' mistresses was the Queen of France, Isabeau of Bavaria, his sister-in-law!

All France was divided between Burgundians and Orléans supporters. Burgundy had the Duke of Orléans murdered but the new Duke's father-in-law, Bernard of Armagnac, took up the fight, and all Frenchmen proclaimed themselves either Burgundians or Armagnacs. In Paris, the university and the butchers were Burgundians, the clergy were Armagnacs. Then, at a meeting to bring reconciliation, the Duke of Burgundy was murdered.

Henry V of England invaded France, and marched from Harfleur across the Somme and into Picardie; at Agincourt, north of Hesdin, he defeated a French army three times the size of his own, killing 10,000 French. Henry, too, was claiming the French throne. Charles VI and his wife married off their daughter Catherine to King Henry V of England, made him regent and heir to the French throne. But this solved the problem only for a short time, as Charles and Henry both died.

Joan of Arc managed to get her beloved Dauphin, son of Charles VI, crowned King, but it was the Burgundians who captured her and sold her to the English. The people of Flanders remained enemies of France for a very long time.

France regained much of Burgundy and Artois around Arras by luck. Charles the Bold, the Duke, was killed in battle and left only a twenty-year-old daughter, Marie. The French seized Burgundy lands on the pretext that as there was no male heir they belonged to the King of France. Then Louis XI tried to marry off his seven-year-old son to Marie. She quickly married the Hapsburg Archduke Maximilian of Austria, and Flanders became part of the Hapsburg Empire. This Empire spread as far as Spain, which led to the crazy situation of what are now Belgium, French Flanders and Dutch Flanders becoming the Spanish Netherlands under the Hapsburg Emperor and Spanish King Charles V. They were separated physically from Spain by France.

Charles's son, Philip II of Spain, who sent the Armada to try to conquer Protestant England, ruthlessly persecuted the Protestant Flemings, leading to constant uprisings over thirty years. When the Catholics of Walloon Flanders and Artois signed a treaty supporting Catholicism and Spain, the Dutch broke away.

In 1660 young Louis XIV, who was twenty-two and in love with the niece of Mazarin, his chief minister, was ordered by Mazarin to marry Maria-Theresa, the daughter of Philip IV of Spain. It was a completely political marriage. As soon as Philip IV died in 1667, without a male heir, Louis claimed the whole of the Netherlands. In 1667 he took Catholic Flanders. A few years before, the French had managed to hold off the Spanish from invading the north of France by winning the Battle of the Dunes, with the considerable help of 8000 of Oliver Cromwell's superbly trained and disciplined English Army, the Ironsides. Cromwell took Dunkerque and kept it. But this time Louis was stopped from advancing further into Belgium and Holland by an alliance of the Protestant countries – England, Holland and Sweden.

The French did finally take Artois in 1676, and Louis XIV's great military engineer Vauban established forts along the new frontier of France from Dunkerque to Lille, Valenciennes and Le Quesnoy and from Gravelines to St Omer, Aire-sur-la-Lys, Béthune, Arras, Douai and Cambrai. The frontier was agreed in 1713 under the Treaty of Utrecht.

Pas de Calais' history has been quite different – ruled entirely by the nearness of England across the English Channel which the French still insist upon calling La Manche – the sleeve. Across this stretch of water, only twenty-two miles wide at its narrowest, the French and English were either constantly at war or were committing acts of piracy against each other, with quite a lot of smuggling thrown in.

Boulogne was the port used by Julius Caesar to invade England in 55 BC.

Calais became English after the great siege of 1346 when the six burghers behaved so bravely (*see* Calais, page 48). That was at the beginning of the Hundred Years War, when Edward III of England was claiming the French throne in the right of his mother, daughter of Philip IV of France. It was the year of the great English victory over the French at Crécy. Calais remained English for 210 years, suffering attacks constantly from the French, who were in Ardres and Boulogne. In 1520 the meeting of François I of France and Henry VIII of England took place at the great Field of the Cloth of Gold outside Guines between Calais and Ardres, but no peaceful alliance came from it.

Calais was finally taken for the French by François de Guise, a great French soldier not to be confused with his son Henri, Duc de Guise, who was largely responsible for the St Bartholomew's Night mass-murder of Protestants. Most of the Calais people were by this time English or certainly English supporters. The French threw them out and re-populated the town with Huguenots fleeing from the Spaniards in Flanders, and refugees from St Quentin, which had been nearly wiped out. The Spaniards then took Calais for two years (1596–8) but it was given to France under the Treaty of Vervins. Calais nearly died as a port after the Treaty of Utrecht because Louis XIV made Dunkerque a free port and it took Calais' trade. Calais became nearly destitute again during the Napoleonic Wars when Napoleon tried to starve out Britain by his Continental System, stopping all trade with Britain by the whole of Europe. The Royal Navy virtually blockaded the Channel. But the smugglers from Calais and Boulogne and from Rye, Winchelsea and Dymchurch ran the blockade of England, and French smuggling was big business.

The English took Boulogne, too. Henry VIII took it in 1544, looted it of everything movable, then sold it back to the French six years later. Napoleon's forces for the invasion of England that never happened were based in Boulogne. On 14 August 1914 the first units of the British Expeditionary Force landed in Boulogne to join the French in fighting the Germans who had invaded Belgium. It was the major port for landing of British troops and equipment in the First World War.

The English held Dunkerque until Charles II, who was always broke because of his great extravagances, sold it back to Louis XIV for five million livres.

All three ports were the lairs of corsairs (pirates licensed by the King). Dunkerque's corsairs had a great notoriety in the days of Jean Bart (1651–1702), who preyed on Dutch, English and

Spanish ships. Bart, son of a Dunkerque fisherman, not only pirated ships but also raided the English coast near Newcastle to loot it. He commanded a small squadron of privateers which attacked a Dutch fleet and rescued a large flotilla of French cornships, escorting them into Dunkerque. He was captured by the English and taken to Plymouth but escaped in a fishing boat (*see* Dunkerque, page 56). Louis XIV received him in honour at Versailles and gave him the command of a naval squadron. He is still a French national hero.

The destruction in Flanders in the First World War was unbelievably appalling. Village after village was destroyed down to the last tree and fence. From the time the German armies crossed into northern France from Belgium in 1914 the destruction got worse and worse, and raged over countryside, villages and towns as far as the Marne and Somme. From there Marshal Foch, Allied Commander-in-Chief, and General Haig, Commander of the British Expeditionary Force, launched the final counter attack which drove the Germans to retreat and surrender in 1918.

The German 'blitzkrieg' advance through Belgium in 1940 was much quicker, but if the damage done to villages and towns by artillery was much less, terrible damage was done by dive-bombers – much of which was totally unnecessary but done deliberately to spread panic and break French morale.

Amiens was one of the worst hit towns and burned furiously. Sixty per cent of it was destroyed. French and British troops stood at Calais, where much of the old town was destroyed, and a great battle was fought around Dunkerque as the British rearguard and French forces held off the German tanks while the Royal Navy, the Merchant Navy and the volunteer 'little ships' from the British coast harbours and resorts miraculously evacuated 350,000 British and French troops from Dunkerque port, the beaches of St Malo-les-Bains and Bray Dunes, under constant artillery fire and dive-bombing. The Somme was no line of defence against the German armour and dive-bombers, though General Weygand tried to hold it and both the British 51st Highland Division and a French Cavalry Regiment did their very best.

Dunkerque, Calais and Boulogne were heavily bombed by

the RAF from 1940 to 1944, but especially when Hitler was planning to invade Britain. Eighty-five per cent of Boulogne was destroyed, though the old walled town around the cathedral on the hill survived. Dunkerque again suffered when the Germans held out there from September 1944 until May 1945. The Germans held out in Calais, too, but the Canadians made a twenty-four-hour truce with them to evacuate civilians. Calais had 17,700 houses in 1939. When it was liberated in 1944 only 660 were near to being intact. British supply boats started to arrive on 20 November 1944. The first French cargo boat docked on 19 July 1945.

Now all three ports have new industries, modern fishing fleets, and all make a very good living from cargo boats and ferries carrying lorries, cars and people to and from Britain.

The north produced two of Europe's greatest medieval historians. Jean Froissart (1333–1405) came from Valenciennes and began to write his *Chronicles* about the wars of his time when he was nineteen. He went to the Courts in England and Scotland and several on the Continent, travelling widely in Germany, Italy and Spain, was with the English Black Prince in Aquitaine, returning to Flanders to complete his writing. From his *Chronicles* historians have learned much of what they know about the period, including the story of the Burghers of Calais and the Battle of Crécy. He was entertaining, dramatic, but accurate in his writing, and very impartial. He also wrote poetry.

Philippe de Commynes (1447–1511), a Fleming, was a statesman who became a historian. He was at the Court of Burgundy but changed to the service of Louis XI of France who rewarded him greatly. But when Louis died, his son Charles VIII was only thirteen years old and Anne, Louis' daughter, ruled as Regent. She purged all Louis' advisers and Commynes was sent for eight months to the notorious 'cages' which Louis had built – iron cages suspended from the ceiling, too small for a man to stand or stretch in. He was then imprisoned until Charles VIII took over and released him. He wrote the first real history as opposed to Froissart's reported descriptions. Both did, however, write the history of their own times, unlike 'the erudite but second-hand historians who succeeded them', as André Maurois said in his *History of France*.

The Flemish painter Pieter Brueghel the Elder (1520–69), who painted so brilliantly scenes of the gusto, the feasting and the horrors of peasant life, was born near Breda in what is now Holland and died in Brussels, though I have seen only one of his pictures in French Flanders.

Amiens

[MAP 2, page 223]

Readers of one of my books were cross with me for routing them through Amiens: just another industrial city with horrific traffic problems, they said. But how can you despise a city of 136,000 people which has made the best velvet in the world since the time of Louis XIV, produces superb chocolate, has a vibrant new university in a challenging modern building and an equally modern concrete and glass Maison de Culture with three theatres, next to a huge sports complex and a cathedral begun in 1220 which is not only the biggest in France but also regarded by many as the finest?

In the First World War, Amiens changed hands between the French and Germans and was bombarded mercilessly in Ludendorff's last great German offensive in 1918; in the Second World War it was set alight by German bombs in 1940, attacked by the RAF, and was more than sixty per cent rubble by 1945. Each time, however, above the rubble, the magnificent Gothic building of the cathedral still stood, crowned by its great spire rising 112 metres, almost unharmed. Not surprisingly, the faithful of Amiens believed that its survival was a miracle, especially as the cathedral was actually hit by nine shells in the First World War.

It is 145 metres long, 70 metres wide at the transept, and has a vault of 43 metres; it is deeply impressive – a masterpiece of northern Gothic art with almost perfectly harmonious proportions. The west face, with two uneven towers, a majestic lacy rose window, and three high arched vaulted doorways, is particularly impressive. Above the portals are great statues of kings, apostles and prophets. Inside, the vast nave, 44 metres long and rather

Amiens Cathedral

solemn, is supported by 126 thin pillars rising to a vaulted roof,
lit quite well by high windows. The famous choir stalls of the
sixteenth century, carved in wood, are absolutely magnificent.
There are 110 of them depicting 3000 domestic and satirical
scenes. At each end of the transept are rose windows, not quite

so fine as the west window above the organ loft. The cathedral was begun in 1220 and mainly completed in fifty years, but the façade and towers took another 200 years. It is in the form of a Latin cross and has seven radiating chapels. John Ruskin, the nineteenth-century essayist, was so impressed by the cathedral that he wrote a guide, which Proust translated into French.

Parts of old Amiens, in quartier St Leu, have survived almost as they were in the Middle Ages, despite being alongside the very modern university. But I understand that there are plans . . . There are old houses by the canal in rue des Granges and rue Motte. Most of the town was redesigned after the Second World War and the 104-metres-tall, twenty-six-storey Tour Perret, opposite the railway station in a rose-flowered square, is a tribute to Auguste Perret, the architect who designed much of it including the railway complex. Le Corbusier's teacher and colleague, he was responsible for the highly controversial building in mass-concrete of the port of Le Havre. He died in 1954. There is a fine view from the top of his heavy tower.

Concrete and glass are the materials of most of the new Amiens, especially the Maison de Culture by Paul Sonrel and the big new university. New industries have come to Amiens, and in its important industrial zone, Longré, are factories for chemicals, tyres, car parts and electronic equipment. But the old textile industry which started in the fifteenth century producing *sayettes* (material of wool serge mixed with silk) still exists and still makes the celebrated *velours d'Amiens* (velvet) introduced in the reign of Louis XIV.

Next to the cathedral, in the seventeenth-century mansion Hôtel de Berny, is a small regional museum with local historic documents and decorative art (open daily except Monday, 1 May to 30 September, then Wednesday, Saturday and Sunday afternoons). The furniture and wood decorations are very good there, especially the charming eighteenth-century woodwork from the Marquis de Lafayette's Château La Grange Bléneau.

The big Musée de Picardie at 42 rue de la République is much more ambitious (open daily except Monday). It was built in Napoleon III's Second Empire with money raised by lotteries. Much of the ground floor is given to archaeology. Many of the items – prehistoric and Gallo-Roman – were found in recent years through aerial photographs. The second-floor paintings include some lovely works, especially in the Flemish section in which Jan van Goyen's landscapes are attractive. Some French eighteenth-century artists feature, such as an outstanding self-portrait by Quentin de la Tour and *The Laundress* by Fragonard, the lively Rococo painter who was almost forgotten after the French Revolution but has become much more appreciated in recent times. There are also good works by Franz Hals, Murillo, Delacroix, Gauguin, Matisse, Jean Lurçat and Rouault, nine interesting decorative hunting scenes by different artists painted between 1736 and 1738 for Louis XV's apartments at Versailles, and a strange group of pictures produced in Amiens from the fifteenth to seventeenth centuries, for a society called Confrérie du Puy Notre-Dame d'Amiens. This society held an annual poetry contest on the theme of the Virgin, then commissioned a painting on the theme for the cathedral. The cathedral became so cluttered that the paintings were taken down in 1723 and many were destroyed. (Museum shut Monday.)

For centuries from the Middle Ages Amiens was famous for its *hortillonnages*. Market gardens still line the network of waterways formed by the Somme but now they sell mostly fruit and flowers. You can hire a boat and buy from waterside stalls. For centuries punts piled high with beautifully fresh vegetables used to be poled to market, but now housewives buy their vegetables the easy way from supermarkets. The growers used to live in wooden chalets on the site. Now these have mostly become weekend bungalows.

Jules Verne, though born in Nantes, lived most of his life in Amiens and is buried in the cemetery of La Madeleine among ornate nineteenth-century tombs. It is difficult to imagine the author of *Voyage to the Centre of the Earth* and *Around the World in Eighty Days* as a local councillor discussing weighty decisions about the drainage. You can visit his house at 2 rue Charles Dubois (tel. 22.45.37.84).

River Somme cruises in the sight-seeing boat *Picardie* include meals – breakfast, lunch or dinner, tea with dancing (Bienvue Picardie, 8 rue Henri IV – 22.92.16.40).

Amiens has a zoo in a green and flowery setting alongside the long man-made lake by Promenade de la Hôtoie.

TOURIST INFORMATION rue Ernest Cauvin
(22.92.26.39); also in place Notre-Dame (15 June–15
September – 22.91.16.16)
MARKETS Daily except Sunday
FESTIVALS Early May – Carnival; June – Picardie Fair-
Exhibition (includes food); mid-June – town fête with
water market

HOTELS

Grand-l'Univers, 2 rue Noyon (22.91.52.51). Fine, small, classic hotel in town centre with big, old rooms. No longer has a restaurant. ROOMS E–F.

Prieuré, 17 rue Porion (22.92.22.47). Little hotel of charm and character in a seventeenth-century house under the shadow of the cathedral. Restaurant, which is gaining popularity for fish and regional dishes, shut Friday evening, Sunday evening. ROOMS C–E. MEALS C–F.

RESTAURANTS

Marissons, 68 rue Marissons (22.92.96.66). In old quarter near the waterside market in an old boatbuilder's workshop from 1486. Excellent cooking with originality. Wide choice of good-value menus. MEALS C–F. Shut 31 December–8 January; 15 July–15 August; Saturday lunch, Sunday evening, Monday.

Mermoz, 7 rue Jean-Mermoz (22.91.50.63). Old favourite, still loved by locals. New décor. Choice of regional or modern dishes. Very good value. MEALS D–F. Shut 1–16 August, Christmas–New Year; Saturday, Sunday evening.

Joséphine, 20 rue Sire-Firmin-Leroux (22.91.47.38). The other local favourite. Classic dishes plus best of the market. MEALS C–F. Shut 7–27 August; Sunday evening, Monday.

Arras

[MAP 5, page 226]

Arras is busy, sometimes crowded but always interesting and, in places, delightful. Its superb Flemish squares surrounded by tall, narrow and elegant houses in old stone and red brick are quite magnificent. Their stepped gables are beautifully ornamented, and their arcades of colonnaded arches make a covered pathway round the squares. Many buildings carry the coats of arms of families or their crafts or trades. You could well believe that they had been there since the sixteenth and seventeenth centuries, and some of them have. The others were rebuilt after the terrible bombardments of the First World War, when major battles were fought round Arras for four years. In 1916 Arras was one of the first towns to suffer a 'mass' bomber raid. Forty German bombers attacked it.

To see just what a splendid job was done by the rebuilders of Arras, drop into the town hall on place des Héros. Just inside on the ground floor are photographs of what Arras looked like in 1918.

The town hall itself, originally fifteenth century, had to be rebuilt, including its superb 75-metre belfry. Place des Héros is a charming square, though the centre is used as a car-park. The cobbled Grand'Place is bigger and blessedly kept free of cars much of the time. There is an underground car-park for 700 cars. Behind arcade pillars are trap doors leading to cellars (*les boves*) several storeys deep – used for storing goods in peace, people in wars.

Both these squares bulge with stalls and people on Saturday when the centuries-old market is held – one of the most colourful in France.

The town hall is interesting. First you meet Colas and Jacqueline – not tourist guides but two of those monumental giants which all self-respecting Flemish towns have possessed since the sixteenth century and which are carried proudly round the town on fête days. Before the Revolution, they often represented

Goliath or St Christopher. Then they became people of local legend or folk heroes. Colas and Jacqueline were two peasant market gardeners who were characters in songs about the defeat and throwing out of the Spaniards in 1654 by the French army of Henri de la Tour d'Auvergne, Vicomte de Turenne. The giants are 6¼ metres high, made originally in 1891, destroyed in 1914 when the Germans took the town for a few weeks, and again in 1940 when the Welsh Guards tried to hold the town against German armour. The present giants were made in 1981. Incidentally, the Welsh Guards were among the British troops to free Arras in August 1944.

Up the main stairs of the town hall in La Salle des Fêtes is an interesting fresco showing life in the sixteenth century. You can see the original twelfth-century cathedral demolished in 1799.

You can reach the top of the superb belfry by climbing all 326 steps or by taking a lift from the vaults and climbing the last thirty-three steep steps. The view from the top is over the rooftops to the cathedral. (The town hall is shut on Sunday afternoon and Monday morning.)

This cathedral is the former church of the ancient abbey of St Vaast (who was the first Bishop), founded in the seventh century. It was built to replace a famous, ancient church in 1766, designed by the architects who built La Madeleine in Paris. It suffered early damage and was not finished until the end of the eighteenth century, but it is a fine piece of classical religious architecture, the colossal monumental staircase leading to it giving it a combined appearance of sober grandeur. The enormous statues of the Saints inside are somewhat out of place. They are nineteenth century, taken from the Panthéon in Paris.

The abbey buildings next to the cathedral, called Palais St Vaast, are equally impressive. The huge cloisters, simply decorated with garlands and roses, are serene despite their size – 50 metres long. Part of the abbey houses the municipal museum. It is a little disappointing because it has only one of the famous Arras tapestries – and even that is disputed. The Arras tapestry industry was at its height in 1384 when the town was within the Duchy of Burgundy. The Burgundian courtiers loved them, and so did their allies of the time, the English. Much of the wool was imported from England, where *arras* became a word for any

tapestry; in *Hamlet* Shakespeare has Polonius hiding behind an
'arras'. Also, *arazzi* is the Italian word for tapestry. The craft was
already dying out in the fifteenth century as the Flemish town of
Tournai (now in Belgium) took over, and ironically the only set
definitely made in Arras that still exists is in Tournai Cathedral.

The museum has some unusual statues, many watercolours
by Dufy, and a good collection of eighteenth-century pottery of
Arras and Tournai (closed Tuesday).

The Citadelle beyond the lower town was built by the military architect Vauban in 1670. Next to it in boulevard Charles de
Gaulle is a British First World War Memorial to the Missing, a
superb colonnade with the central monument dedicated to the
Royal Flying Corps, Royal Naval Service and Royal Air Force. It
records 35,928 names of the missing from the battles around
Arras, including the terrible fighting at Vimy Ridge, 8km NE
(*see* Vimy Ridge, page 214). When I was young, Arras was a
great centre of pilgrimage for people visiting the First World
War battlefields. Now the Normandy beaches are the centre of
such pilgrimages – another generation and another war.

Down a narrow road beside the war memorial is the Mur des
Fusilés with plaques recording the names of 200 French Resistance fighters shot there by the Germans in the Second World

War. The Arras Resistance movement was very strong. One of its leaders was the man who was teacher in English at Arras Lycée, the Socialist Guy Mollet, later one of the originators of the Treaty of Rome which founded the European Community, and President of the Consultative Assembly of Europe in 1955. He was French Prime Minister 1956–7. But he is remembered in Arras as its Deputé (MP) and Mayor from 1945–75 and the man responsible for rebuilding Arras economically, industrially and physically. The A26 motorway, which goes near to Calais and Boulogne, now runs within 6km of the town, joining the A1 motorway Lille–Paris only 7km NE. It has put Arras on the main routes of Europe, including routes to the Tunnel.

There is still a rue Robespierre in Arras, and a bust of him in the town hall. He was born there in 1758, of Irish origin. His father, grandfather and Maximilian de Robespierre himself were all lawyers. He became public prosecutor for Artois. Yet he was also a poet. In the French Revolution he led the extremist wing, the Jacobins, against the Liberal intellectual Girondists, so called because most of their leaders came from Bordeaux. The Jacobins won, the King and Queen were executed, the guillotine worked overtime all over France. It was the time of the Terror. Gradually Robespierre became dictator. But he overplayed his hand, was outlawed by his own party and guillotined in 1794. 'He entertained the fearful certitude of a man who believes he has a mission,' wrote Maurois later, and such men – or women – are dangerous.

TOURIST INFORMATION 7 place Mar.-Foch
(21.51.26.95)
MARKETS Thursday, Saturday, Sunday morning
FESTIVALS May – Procession Notre-Dame; June – Fête
de l'Été; 25 August – Fête d'Arras.

HOTELS

Chanzy, 8 rue Chanzy (21.71.02.02). My old favourite. The de Troyes family have retired after fifty years but new owners stick to classic and Flemish cooking. Loved by locals. Superbly stocked wine-cellar. ROOMS C–D. MEALS C–F.

Univers, 3 place Croix-Rouge (21.71.34.01). In eighteenth-century monastery. Elegant. Regional dishes. ROOMS C–F. MEALS C–F.

Trois Luppars, 47 Grande Place (21.07.41.41). In lovely fifteenth-century house, good modern rooms. Run by Mme de Troyes (ex-Chanzy). No restaurant. ROOMS C–F. Eat at Faisanderie next door.

RESTAURANTS

Faisanderie, 45 Grande Place (21.48.20.76). Jean-Pierre Dargent moved from Pommera to historic house here. Superb cooking. MEALS E–G. Shut February holidays, 6–27 August; Sunday evening, Monday.

Ambassadeur (Buffet Gare), (21.23.29.80). Has lost its Michelin star but is still one of the best station buffets in Europe. MEALS C–F. Shut Sunday evening.

Boulogne

[MAP 5, page 226]

Henry VIII of England captured Boulogne and today you could be forgiven for thinking that he never sold it back to the French.

More than three million Britons invade the port each year, so it is almost always crowded, noisy, chaotic and, to me, still great fun. Many one-day visitors are gone by 6 p.m. and many are passing through, but enough stay to give Boulogne a distinctly Anglo-French look and sound. The ticking cash registers console the Boulonnais considerably, and save them following the tradition of their ancestors who popped over the Channel on visits to British fishing villages to collect money and food supplies, not to mention souvenirs such as church silver and women. Between times, they robbed English and Dutch ships. Modern British invaders may sometimes be noisy and drunken, but they do pay for the loot they take home!

In 1377 the Boulonnais sacked and burned Rye, so the incensed Sussex Cinq Port fishermen sacked Boulogne. Napoleon spent three years there preparing to invade England. He built 2000 flat-bottomed boats and a memorial column to his Grande Armée – a premature victory column. When he heard of Nelson's win at Trafalgar, he headed west for Austerlitz next day. In 1941 Hitler collected invasion barges in Boulogne harbour while he contemplated Dover's cliffs from the same clifftop at Cap Gris Nez as Napoleon had done in 1801. RAF bombing raids on the barges destroyed nearly all Boulogne's port. As one of the RAF airmen who did it, I am deeply pleased that we missed almost completely the precious Ville Haute, although I cannot claim that it was not partly luck. We did go rather uncomfortably low to do it.

Boulogne is above all a fishing port with 100,000 tons landed in a year – and it begins for me at quai Gambetta where fish is sold from stalls until about midday. That is the place to buy oysters, truly fresh sole or the famous Boulogne mussels to take home in a plastic bag before you drive across the bridge to the ferry port. The new wholesale fish market hall is now over the river.

Quai Gambetta is the place to park. Though the hill up to the Ville Haute is steep, there is little point in driving. You won't find anywhere to park up there. Quai Gambetta ends at Pont Marguet which you cross to reach the ferry. Opposite, on the corner of the rue Faidherbe, is Hamiot's brasserie, known to locals and British habitués since the Second World War. The Hamiots have not run it for five years but it remains the place where fishermen wash the salt out of their mouths at the bar in early morning, and the rest of the day waiters dart around at high speed to a background of chatter, serving plate after plate of mussels, plaice, sole, shrimps and dozens more dishes, all with hillocks of *frites*, those gourmet fried potatoes which bear little relation to American French fries or British chips.

Walk past rue Faidherbe and the post office to Grande-rue.

Be warned – it is full of tempting shops and side-streets leading
to shops and café-restaurants. Leave them until you come down
from the old town.

On the way up you pass the old St Nicholas Church in place
Dalton. Each Wednesday and Saturday morning in this little
square there is a delightful market for butter, pâté, cheese and
vegetables brought from the farm that morning, chickens, cider

and colourful flowers. Opposite the church is the now famous little Brasserie Alfred, a true old French bistro – crowded, often noisy, serving wonderful shellfish and trenchermen meals. It was once my private hideaway. Now you must get there shortly after midday in high season to get a table. Jules (*see* Restaurants, below) is two doors away, in the oldest house in Boulogne, though its new plasticky façade has ruined that.

Up the hill at the old town walls, turn right along the flower-lined boulevard to Porte des Degrés – the gate shut from Henry VIII's siege in 1544 until 1895 and even now open only to pedestrians. From here you can mount the thirteenth-century ramparts and walk along them. The view is superb, both down into Ville Haute and across the port. The ramparts are surprisingly wide, with shady gardens and lawns – a favourite stroll for local people, with children playing on their grassy slopes. A quiet stroll round them, admiring the views, would take about forty-five minutes, though you could nip round in twenty minutes. You can walk up the ramparts from any of the four town gates which are flanked with two towers – Portes Gayolle, des Dunes, de Calais and des Degrés. In places you can see right down into the château which is divided from the walls by a moat. It was built in 1231 on Roman foundations by Philippe-le-Hurepel, son of King Philippe Auguste and Count of Boulogne. His name, it seems, meant Philippe the Impolite! This castle was strengthened so successfully in the sixteenth century by Louis XIV's military architect Vauban that in 1940 Hitler's 2nd Panzer Division failed to take it. The French garrison walked out with flying colours when France capitulated. Unfortunately for archaeologists, Philippe had used much of the old Roman fortifications in building the castle. Prince Louis Napoleon, future Emperor Napoleon III, was imprisoned in it in 1840 after an abortive effort to oust King Louis Philippe. After the First World War, the body of the British Unknown Warrior lay there in state on its way to burial in Westminster Abbey. The château is being restored by the town (1991) and will soon house the Greek vases, other ceramics and Egyptian treasures from the museum (*see* Museum, below).

Inside the ramparts dominating the old town is the Cathedral of Notre-Dame, its Italianate dome visible from countryside and sea. It was built between 1827 and 1866 on the site of previous churches dating back to AD636. It seems that in that year a statue of the Virgin, standing in a boat, was pushed ashore by angels. Louis XI pronounced it a true Madonna in 1477, though God only knows how he could tell. Pilgrims flocked to the cathedral. Fourteen French kings and five Kings of England came to pray, as well as evildoers and murderers seeking to absolve their sins.

In the vast crypt, with many rooms and passages, Edward II of England married Isabelle, daughter of Philippe IV of France, in 1308. Their son, Edward III, claimed the French throne and started the Hundred Years War. Henry VIII's soldiers later stole cathedral treasures and burned records. Then Calvinists made a bonfire of the Virgin's statue. The next statue was burned in the French Revolution and its replacement was stolen in 1830, turning up in 1850 without its boat or angels. The present statue was designed in twelfth-century style by a local sculptor Paul Graf in 1924. In mid-August, fishermen, farmers and girls in traditional headgear walk in procession uphill to pay homage.

The Italian dome, decorated by Vatican craftsmen, is superb from inside and out. It has been called a synthesis of the Pantheon in Rome, Aux Invalides in Paris and London's St Paul's. It has also been called ill-proportioned. Remarkable, too, are the statue of St Joseph made from one enormous block of Carrara marble and the white marble altar made in nine sections but joined with settings of 150 precious stones so that it looks like one single piece. The altar's biblical figures are carved in incredible detail. It arrived in Boulogne in 1866 and my old French guidebooks say that it was a present from an English girl named Laughan in memory of her parents. Modern guidebooks say that it was a present from an Italian prince and arrived in sections on ornate wagons pulled by thirty-six white stallions – a far better story.

Place Godefroy Bouillon, centre of Ville Haute, is named after a local man who led the first Crusade and was made King of Jerusalem but refused 'to wear a crown of gold where my Saviour wore a crown of thorns', and called himself 'Defender of the Holy Sepulchre'.

All that remains of the old Count's palace is the grey stone Gothic thirteenth-century belfry tower, 45 metres tall, next to the contrasting elegant eighteenth-century town hall in rose brick. The public library opposite was a pilgrims' rest house, a hospital, a convent, then a prison in the Revolution. You can go into its charming cloistered garden.

When planning to invade England between 1802 and 1804, Napoleon used as headquarters the Desandrovins mansion opposite the town hall, now grandly named Imperial Palace. He returned in 1810 with his young wife Marie Louise and, ever the optimist, sent Maréchal Ney to prepare again to invade.

Round the old walls are seventeen towers. As you leave by Porte des Dunes you see Gayette tower. A wall plaque tells of another optimist – Pilatre de Rozier. Having been one of the first humans to fly with Marquis d'Arlande in the Montgolfier hot-air balloon over Paris in 1783, he tried two years later from this tower to cross the Channel to Dover. Colonel Jean-Pierre Blanchard and an American Dr John Jeffries beat him to the crossing in a hydrogen balloon, but they flew from Dover to near Calais. Rozier reached 550 metres then his balloon collapsed. He and his companion Romain are buried in nearby Wimille churchyard. In Guines Forest is a column to the men who made it across, Blanchard and Jeffries.

Walking down Grande-rue to the port you pass, at No. 34, the museum in a seventeenth-century building. The remarkable collection of Greek, Roman and Egyptian treasures are to be transferred soon to the château, but the collection of paintings is to remain. It includes works by Boudin, Corot, Fantin-Latour and Auguste Delacroix (1807–60), who painted local maritime life and costumes. There is a statue of Stephen, twelfth-century King of England before Henry II, first Plantagenet, known locally as Étienne de Blois, Comte de Boulogne. And there is Napoleon's hat! Napoleon was very careless with his hats, which he left all over France, including one at Moët et Chandon Champagne cellars in Épernay. He must have drunk more than Wellington, who took his hat with him. In the museum you can also see what British cartoonists of the time thought of Napoleon's 'invasion' fiasco.

Grande-rue, rue Faidherbe running parallel, and the side-streets off them, such as Victor Hugo, Thiers and Lampe, are always thick with traffic and people, for most of the shops are here, and Boulogne is a good shopping centre for almost anything except high fashion, though there are some women's clothes shops in rue Nationale. For expensive conserves, from jams to *confits* of goose, La Comtesse du Barry delicatessen at 35 Grande-rue is fashionable. Derrien in Grande-rue is a good charcuterie, open Sunday mornings. But the great shop of Boulogne is Philippe Olivier's now-famous cheese shop in rue Thiers where he not only sells more than 200 different cheeses from dairies, factories and from farms all over France, but he matures them at appropriate temperatures in his three cellars. There are a few foreign cheeses. Stilton represents England. Occasionally lucky visitors are shown round the cellars. The smell is both delicious and head-reeling. Philippe used to help in the *épicerie* started by his grandfather in Dieppe – still run by the family and famous for cheese.

For a wine, make for Le Chais, a wine-cellar formerly wholesale only, now a splendid place to buy a bottle, your duty-free allowance or a few cases. Buy a better quality wine and you will still be in pocket after paying British customs duty and VAT. To find it, drive up boulevard Daunau (left just past the post office when driving from the fish quai). After going under the railway bridge turn very sharp left into rue Deux Ponts. (Alas, Le Chais is shut on Sunday and Monday.)

Boulogne inevitably has good fish restaurants (*see* below). Past the fishing port along boulevard Sainte Beuve (named after a local man) was the post-1945 casino, descendant of one opened in 1863, very fashionable when Napoleon III frequented it. The casino is being replaced by a glasshouse called 'Nausicea', an unfortunate name for the National Centre of the Sea. Due to be opened in May 1991, it will have permanent shows of a tropical lagoon, marine life in cold seas, a large, deep tank for observing fish behaviour, a huge tank for sharks, and another for scientific testing of fishing boats. It will also have a big restaurant and swimming-pool. It is beside a big sand beach where, in summer, stalls serve anything from *frites* to a lunch of steak or fish. It is used mostly by French families. But once the beach was English territory, discovered by them very soon after Dieppe. The fun-loving, eccentric Duchess of Barry, whose son should have been Charles IV of France if his uncle Louis-Philippe had not grabbed the throne when Charles was a boy, made the old English custom of sea-bathing fashionable with the French. After the Napoleonic Wars, and especially after the Casino opened, the English flocked to Boulogne, many of them to live there.

In 1842 it was reported that one in six of Boulogne's 30,000 inhabitants were British, and it may have been more, for a lot were virtually in hiding. Many were couples 'living in sin', which meant total ostracism in Victorian society unless, of course, you were a prince. Others were bankrupts, avoiding their creditors and a debtors' prison. Some had been chased to Dover or the three-mile limit by officers of the court. Boulogne's shop-keepers, restaurants and hotels soon found that they were not cured of their bad habits, and so many British were in the debtors' prison in Grande-rue last century that it was called 'L'Hôtel Angleterre'! But other Britons were fairly rich and Boulogne became fashionable, so Parisians built elegant houses there – mostly destroyed, alas, in the Second World War.

Charles Dickens was often in Boulogne. He stayed in Condette, a village in the woods near Hardelot, at the villa of his local friend Beaucourt-Mutuel and there wrote parts of *Hard Times* and *Bleak House*. Officially he went to take the sea air but a young actress called Ellen Ternan also inspired him to deep breathing. Les Amis de Charles Dickens Society still meets there.

Napoleon's marble column to his Grande Armée was finished for him by King Louis-Philippe (1830–48), 'the Citizen King', who, when thrown out by the citizens, fled to England and lived as 'Mr Smith' in Surbiton. Napoleon's statue is in bronze, with his back to the Channel and England – towards Austerlitz, no doubt. It is 5km north of Boulogne on the N1. Climb the 265 steps to get a splendid panoramic view, some days even to the white cliffs of Dover.

2km north on the D240 Wimereux road is a stone where, in 1804, Napoleon gave away his second batch of Legion of Honour decorations – 2000 of them. He also struck a medal for his soldiers inscribed: '*Descente en Angleterre, frappé à Londres*' (Descent on England – strike at London). However, at the request of the townspeople, his troops were camped on the hillsides and were not allowed into Boulogne.

The impressive cross on the hill way above the beach is Calvaire des Marins, dedicated to sailors lost in shipwrecks or wars.

Boulogne has a very large supermarket, the Continent, on the corner of boulevard Daunou, with a big multi-storey car-park and an Auchan hypermarket 7km towards St Omer.

TOURIST INFORMATION quai de la Poste, between
Marguet bridge and the post office (21.31.68.38)
MARKETS Wednesday, Saturday. Fish daily in the
morning except Sunday
FESTIVALS Last Saturday, Sunday in August –
Pilgrimage of Notre-Dame; last Sunday in June – Swan
Festival with street market; mid-August – Summer
Carnival; first Saturday in December–Santa Claus
arrives: street celebration

HOTELS

Plage, 124 boul. Ste-Beuve (21.31.45.35). Rooms simple, pleas-ant; front rooms noisy in summer. Very good-value meals. Super fish. ROOMS B–C. MEALS A–D. Shut Christmas–15 January.
Faidherbe, 12 rue Faidherbe (21.31.60.93). Bed and breakfast. Pleasant. Front rooms noisy. ROOMS D–E.
Métropole, 51 rue Thiers (21.31.54.30). Very agreeable. Bed and breakfast. ROOMS C–E. Shut 20 December–5 January.

RESTAURANTS

Brasserie Alfred, 24 place Dalton (21.31.53.16). Lively old-style bistro. Not for snobs or tête-à-tête meals. Excellent shellfish. MEALS C–F. Shut 22 December–5 January.
Chez Jules, 10 place Dalton (21.31.54.12). Bar-brasserie in oldest house in Boulogne, once full of young French, who still go to

buy hamburgers. Tables mostly taken by British. Stays open very late. MEALS B–D.

Matelote, 80 boul. Ste-Beuve (21.30.17.97). Best fish restaurant in area. Fairly modern, individual dishes. Excellent desserts. MEALS D–G. Book. Shut 15–30 June; 23 December–15 January; Sunday evening.

Liégeoise, 10 rue Monsigny (21.31.61.15). Old favourite revived. Light modern cooking. Used by local businessmen. MEALS F–G. Shut 15–31 July; Sunday evening, Wednesday.

Huitrière, 11 place Lorraine (21.31.35.27). Good fish shop off rue Faidherbe with a few tables – superb simple fish dishes with white wine. MEALS C–G. Shut Sunday evening, Monday.

See also Pont-de-Briques, page 182 (5km S by D940).

Calais

[MAP 5, page 226]

The first time I took a car to Calais it was hoisted aboard the ferry at Folkstone by a crane and hoisted off at Calais, hitting the quayside with a suspension-testing bump. Then Calais was the first port to introduce mobile ramps, leading to a spectacular rise in cross-Channel motor traffic. Now Calais handles more than two million vehicles each year and nine million passengers – three times as many as Boulogne. If Calais appears to be less crowded with Britons, there are two reasons. Firstly, Calais is much bigger, with nearly 80,000 inhabitants against Boulogne's 45,000, so the visitors are less conspicuous. Secondly, the modern ferry-port is well away from the main town and direction signs steer you around the outside of the town in an apparent effort to get rid of you as soon as possible. I assume that the people are too busy looking after their extensive commercial and industrial affairs to look after very many visitors, for it is an industrial town as well as an important port, handling many cargoes, including wood from the Soviet Union and chemicals for industry. As the Channel Tunnel gets into full operation, much of the ferry traffic will bypass the port, which is why the wise burghers of Calais are already enlarging their commercial port and making a deep-water basin to take ships of up to 60,000 tons.

British visitors would spend a lot more time in Calais if they got to know it better. Mostly, they do their shopping around place d'Armes or just up rue Royale as far as Hotel Meurice, an area where the shops and restaurants exist almost entirely for their benefit. They rarely explore past the town hall. They know nothing of the true old-style French shops on the 'other town' at the top of the hill or of the market in place Crèvecoeur, and never dream of resting on the big, pleasant sandy beach at the other end of town.

Calais' destiny has been ruled by its nearness to England – just 38km. Back in the fourteenth century, it was known to English merchants as a sinister haunt of pirates. When Edward III of England invaded France to claim the French crown, and, unwittingly, start the Hundred Years War, he eventually took Calais after an eight-month siege starting September 1346. In the Middle Ages it was usual at the end of a long siege for successful attackers to kill off the defending citizens for having caused too much trouble. In Calais six burghers, leading citizens of the town, offered their lives to Edward III as sacrifice if he would spare the ordinary citizens. He agreed, but his wife Philippa of Hainault, a Fleming, pleaded for the lives of the six and Edward spared them, too. Outside Calais town hall, which was rebuilt in fifteenth-century style from 1911–23, is Auguste Rodin's famous and splendid statue in bronze of the six burghers. He was asked to do it in 1885, made three maquettes in different designs, and completed the final design in 1895. It is regarded as probably Rodin's greatest work – but the city fathers of Calais did not like it at the time. Now even the maquettes have pride of place in Calais Museum at 25 rue Richelieu.

The English stayed in Calais for 210 years, using it as a port, especially for wool, and a military camp. Nearly all the French people were driven out or left and were replaced by English.

Rodin's Burghers of Calais

The French attacked it from Boulogne and Ardres and the English retaliated with raids of looting and sacking. It cost England a fortune in money and resources to hold it. It was from Calais that Henry VIII set out to meet François I at their great summit called 'The Field of the Cloth of Gold' (*see* Guines, page 143).

The English built the church of Notre-Dame near place

d'Armes in English Perpendicular style. That was where Général de Gaulle was married in 1921 to the daughter of the Mayor of Calais.

In 1558 a French army under a great soldier Duc François de Guise, father of the Catholic leader who organized the St Bartholomew's Day Massacre and who plotted to get the French throne, took Calais for the French. The English inhabitants were thrown out and replaced with Huguenot refugees from Flanders fleeing from Spanish occupation and from St Quentin, which had been destroyed when the Spanish defeated the French there a year earlier. The newcomers were lured with bargain-priced land. After the Treaty of Utrecht, when the French invasion into Flanders had been halted and the northern frontiers of France were agreed, Louis XIV was anxious to please the Flemings within France and granted special tax concessions to Dunkerque which made it virtually a free port, so Calais' trade died. Its population dropped to 6000. It is strange that after the Second World War Paris once again poured money into Dunkerque and Boulogne for rebuilding, while Calais had to borrow where it could, and sought help from British companies.

In the Napoleonic Wars Calais suffered again when Napoleon forbade trade with Britain and the British fleet held the Channel. Calais sailors took to piracy as corsairs. The most famous was Thomas Sonville, who made a fortune in prize-money.

The village of St Pierre (now Calais Sud) has become entirely separated from Calais. It was there that some Nottingham lace-makers came to set up workshops after the defeat of Napoleon in 1815. They came illegally, for there was still a death penalty for anyone in England who exported the know-how of manufacture. Calais' lace industry became world famous and still exists, flourishing or not according to fashions. At present it flourishes. The reason for the expansion of lace-making was that in 1830 the mechanic from Lyon, Joseph Jacquard, invented a loom which enabled ordinary workmen to make silk with beautiful patterns in a style which previously took hours of skill by artists. An Englishman, Ferguson, adapted it for use in lace-making. Jacquard's name has entered the world of textiles and fashions.

His statue in bronze stands in front of Calais' theatre, a building renovated inside so successfully in 1986 that it is second only in importance to the Lille theatre in the north of France.

The British returned to Calais in the nineteenth century. As in Boulogne, many were running from creditors. Emma Lyon died in poverty and misery in 1815 at No. 27 rue Française. She was Nelson's Lady Hamilton, hiding at a farmhouse in St Pierre under her maiden name. She had fled England owing £18,000 – a fair sum in those days. But the captains of all the English vessels in Calais went to her funeral.

Another who lived in Calais to avoid his creditors and the wrath of the Prince Regent, who had tired of his barbed wit, was Beau Brummell, 'king' of Bath and Tunbridge Wells, arbiter of fashion and manners in high society but addicted to gambling. He stayed in Calais for fifteen years under his first names of George Bryan, then went to Caen as British vice-consul, a job gained for him by old friends which he then lost, went to prison for debt, was saved by French friends, and died in a mean hotel planning big parties to which nobody came.

A happier Briton living in Calais was the Nottingham painter Richard Parkes Bonington, the brilliant water-colourist who specialized in landscapes with remarkable use of light effects, particularly in skies. Alas, he died of sunstroke at the age of twenty-six. Some of his landscapes are in the Calais Museum.

In May 1940 French and British troops made a stand in the harbour area. The Green Jackets (the Rifle Brigade) made a last stand in the sixteenth-century citadel and on a tiny island in the harbour. Sadly the whole of the old part of Calais nearby was burned down by the Germans – some say deliberately. Now its centre, place d'Armes, is a square with uninspired modern buildings where visitors go shopping. Dull roads lead to empty building lots and the big ferry terminal.

The thirteenth-century Watch Tower in place d'Armes, Tour du Guet, was damaged but has been very well repaired. It was used early last century as a telegraph station and from there the news of the death of Napoleon was transmitted via a chain of telegraphs to Paris. Before 1940 it was entirely surrounded by ancient houses. Now the square is a car-park except on market days (Wednesday and Saturday mornings). You can cross to the citadel on a bridge and behind the gates is a peaceful garden and a sports field. There is a little war museum in a German bunker once used as a German navy control centre in parc St Pierre.

Rue Royale, which runs from place d'Armes towards the station and town hall, has the better hotels and pricier shops, including Au Gourmet charcuterie and Leonadis chocolates. Maison de Fromage in rue Gerschell, opposite place d'Armes, sells 200 cheeses but is not in the class of Olivier in Boulogne.

Straight on from Royale past the railway station and town hall is boulevard Jacquard where you will find banks and the shops that most locals use, including Printemps and Prisunic department stores, Fin Bec for cheese and wine and Fonteyne for super ladies' underwear. By the casino, turn left into boulevard Lafayette. Just off it is place Crèvecoeur where a big market is held on Thursday and Saturday (good for butter, cheese, vegetables and fish).

The road that goes the other way from place d'Armes leads over a mobile bridge to the big sandy beach. Until the mid-1930s this was a military zone and nothing could be built beside it except wooden buildings which could be dismantled in twenty-four hours. So only in recent years has it become a bathing beach, with a good restaurant, Côte d'Argent, and small apartment blocks in gardens. The beach runs into Blériot Plage from which Blériot made the first cross-Channel flight in 1909.

Calais has two hypermarkets – Continent 2½km east and Mammoth 3km west, both served by buses from the ferry-port.

TOURIST INFORMATION 12 boul. Clemenceau
(21.96.62.40) (Shut Sunday except July, August)
MARKETS Thursday, Saturday in place Crèvecoeur;
Wednesday, Saturday mornings near place d'Armes
FESTIVALS Second fortnight July – fair-exhibition of La
Côte d'Opale; last weekend in May – big flea-market,
Les Puces Calaisiennes

HOTELS

George V, 36 rue Royale (21.97.68.00). The Beauvalot family from La Bretagne, St Omer, have renovated this old hotel; very good now. Gastronomic restaurant and a bistro with good-value cheap menu. ROOMS C–E. MEALS A (bistro), D–E. Restaurant shut 23 December–3 January; Saturday lunch, Sunday evening.

Meurice, 5 rue Édouard Roche, off rue Royale (21.34.57.03). Most comfortable in Calais. Founded in 1772 by local postmaster Augustine Meurice to serve London–Paris coach passengers. He founded a string of hotels, ending with the Meurice in Paris – one of France's most famous hotels. Restaurant independent – see Diligence. ROOMS E–F.

Windsor, 2 rue Cdt Bonningue (21.34.59.40). Friendly, useful, on road to ferry. Some rooms simple. No restaurant. ROOMS B–E.

Holiday Inn, boul. Alliés (21.34.69.69). New in 1989, near place d'Armes. ROOMS G. MEALS D–E.

RESTAURANTS

Channel, 3 boul. Résistance (21.34.42.30). Established local and British favourite. Excellent fish. MEALS B–F. Shut 5–15 June; 20 December–20 January; Sunday evening, Monday.

Diligence, 7 rue Édouard Roche (21.96.92.89). At Hotel Meurice but independent. Cheaper menus good value. MEALS C–F. Shut Sunday, Monday lunch.

Coq d'Or, 31 place d'Armes (21.34.79.05). Good value for bourgeois cooking. Good choice on several menus. MEALS A–F. Shut Wednesday.

Salons Rodin, rue Fleurs near theatre (21.36.56.20). New but run by a family in the restaurant business for nine generations. Good cheap menus and carte. MEALS B–F. Shut 15 July–15 August; Sunday evening, Monday.

Dunkerque

[MAP 6, page 227]

Poor Dunkerque has had a hard life. It changed hands many times between warring nations, finally taking a terrible beating in 1940 when eighty per cent of it was wiped out. Its port is completely new and is the third largest in France. It takes giant oil tankers and container ships, as well as ferries from Britain, and it has a busy naval dockyard. It does look like a concrete desert at times, but the port is a few miles west of the town, which makes the town itself cosier and more peaceful, though it is inconvenient for day-trippers coming from Ramsgate in Kent by Sally Line boats. As a result, most motorists crossing on their way to Paris or further south skirt the town to reach the A25 motorway and do not see it, which is a pity, for though not pretty it has a pleasant ambience, is lively and very Flemish. Until 1970 the beach-resort of Dunkerque was a separate little town – Malo-les-Bains – reached by bridges across the Wateringues canal. It was from the huge sand beach and dunes starting at Malo and stretching to Bray Dunes that British and French troops were evacuated in 1940 by a great motley fleet of warships, merchantmen and little ships from the harbours of Kent and Essex under constant shellfire and dive-bombing from the Germans. The British command had estimated that they could evacuate 45,000. In fact, 338,326 were rescued. The boats that took the troops off the beaches included lifeboats from liners in London docks, Thames tugs, lighters, barges, fishing boats and pleasure yachts. 860 boats took part in the evacuation. Two thirds of the troops were taken from Dunkerque's harbour, a third from the sand beaches. It could not have been done if British and French troops had not fought to hold a line from Gravelines to Bergues and along the canal to Nienpont in Belgium. On the eighth and final day, 4 June 1940, 4000 British troops and several thousand French were fighting the rearguard. They fought until overwhelmed right in Dunkerque town.

In 1944 the German Admiral Frisius commanding the troops

occupying Dunkerque flooded the Moëres valley to the south-east as a barrier and held the post against the Canadians until Germany capitulated in May 1945.

Malo is not pretty but has some excellent fish restaurants along its promenade. It is becoming a residential area and lures thousands of people from Lille on summer weekends. Until the seventh century, the site where Dunkerque now stands was a dangerous sandbank just under the sea. When the sea receded, St Eloi built a chapel in the dunes and a settlement of fishermen grew up. Not until 1067 did the name Dunkerque (Church of the Dunes) appear. Dunkerque was part of Flanders which came unwillingly under Spanish rule as a part of the Spanish Nether-lands (*see* History, page 23). When the Spanish Armada sailed to attack England in 1588, the Spanish had turned Dunkerque into an important military base. A huge Spanish army was waiting there under the command of the Duke of Parma. He had 200 flat-bottomed boats to transport his soldiers to England. His problem was that the galleons of the Armada could not sail into the shallow waters around Dunkerque (the Banks of Seeland) and Parma could not bring out his cumbersome unarmed trans-ports because of the Dutch, who had small but well-gunned ships with shallow draughts waiting to sink the transports. Some-one in Madrid had blundered. In trying to get as near as possible to the sandbanks, the Spanish galleons gave themselves very little room for manoeuvre which exposed them to English fire-ships. The wind was blowing them closer to the treacherous sandbanks. Luckily for them they were saved by a sudden shift of wind direction.

In 1658 the Spanish were driven out of much of Flanders. A combined force of Oliver Cromwell's remarkable Army, the Ironsides, and the French under Turenne defeated the Spanish conclusively at the Battle of the Dunes. Dunkerque surrendered to the English who kept the town.

When Charles II became king of England, he was soon desperately short of money and decided that Dunkerque was too costly to maintain so far from England, so he sold it to the French in 1662 for five million crowns.

Under William and Mary, the English got together with the Dutch to stop the French going any further into Flanders, and

Dunkerque found itself just inside the French frontier, as it is now. Louis XIV did all he could to keep the local Flemings happy, giving them rights to tax-free imports and exports which made Dunkerque prosper at the expense of Calais.

Before France was even at war with England and Holland, the corsairs of Dunkerque were attacking their ships, especially the Dutch. They captured 3000 ships and took 30,000 crew prisoners, almost destroying Holland's seaborne trade. The hero of these corsairs was Jean Bart (1651–1702). Louis XIV not only turned a blind eye to his piracy but also gave him command of a squadron. He is still a French hero, particularly in Dunkerque where his statue, by David d'Angers, stands in the main square which is called after him. He is buried here in St Eloi church. In and around the square is the main shopping centre.

The tower across the road from the church belonged to a previous church of 1440, burned down in 1558. It has a carillon of forty-eight bells which play *La Cantale de Jean Bart* every hour. You can go up it on afternoons in July and August. The Syndicat d'Initiative (tourist information centre) is on the ground floor.

The town hall, built in 1900, has a belfry 75 metres high. From its balcony the mayor throws smoked herrings to the crowd on the Sunday before Lent – the last day of the Carnival when the people dress up and walk in lively procession round the town. In the procession Dunkerque's traditional giants get an airing (*see* Lille, page 61). The top giant is a Scandinavian warrior called Reuze – said to be a Viking raider who was wounded. Instead of killing him the locals nursed him to health, so he stayed to defend them. It seems that he did the same for Cassel!

The smoked herrings which the Mayor throws are called 'Les Kippers' very loudly by the crowd calling for them but are more like our bloaters than our kippers. The carnival goes on for a whole month and is great fun. I went recently to one of the balls, an all-action fancy-dress affair which went on for most of the night. Champagne was swallowed at the rate of beer at a rugby-club dance, but I did not see one fight or one punch thrown.

The carnival was originally for the fishermen. Dunkerque

still has a fishing fleet which docks in the old port in the heart of town, and you can buy from stalls on the quayside.

There has been an attempt to instil some culture into the town with two modern art galleries, but the critics are mostly unimpressed. The new Musée des Beaux Arts is in a heavy concrete building imitating Le Corbusier and is interesting rather than impressive. Its paintings (sixteenth to twentieth centuries) include French Baroque and Rococo works, plus *A View of Dunkerque* by Corot (1796–1875), and works by landscape and figure artists. There are paintings by Maurice Marinot (1882–1962), one of the Fauves group of which Matisse was the greatest exponent. They were known for the bold use of very colourful paint. Better is the case of Marinot's gorgeously delicate glass-work. The ground floor has models of early ships, and paintings of Dunkerque history and personalities. There is a large painting of the old port by Isabey (1767–1855), Napoleon's favourite artist, known mostly for his miniatures. In the basement are photos and documents of Dunkerque's part in the Second World War.

The Contemporary Art Museum is in a specially built sculpture park. You walk around grassy slopes passing at intervals stone and twisted-metal shapes – modern sculptures. Inside are modern works by such artists as the abstract expressionist Sam Francis and pop artist Andy Warhol. A room is devoted to the Dutch artist Karel Appel who said that he painted like a barbarian in a barbaric world. He is now known for colourful wooden reliefs rather like children's toys. A modern amphitheatre is used for experimental ballet and other performances. Both museums are shut on Tuesday.

You can visit the lighthouse (*phare*). Climb the 238 steps and there are wonderful views of ships, the town, port and Malo beach.

TOURIST INFORMATION Beffroi (28.66.79.21), and 488
Digue de Mer, Malo-les-Bains (28.63.20.60)
MARKETS Wednesday, Saturday
FESTIVALS The month before Lent – carnival; August
–Fête de Mer

HOTELS

Dunkerque

Europ Hotel, Mareyeur Restaurant, 13 rue Leughenaer (28.66.29.07). Large, businessmen's hotel. Restaurant meals excellent value. Good fish and shellfish. Also grill. ROOMS E. MEALS C. Restaurant shut Sunday.

Altéa Reuze, 2 rue J-Jaures (28.59.11.11). Views over port and town. By Tour de Reuze. Rooms quite pricey. ROOMS E–G. MEALS A–D.

Malo-les-Bains

Hirondelle, 46 ave Faidherbe (28.63.17.65). Nice little hotel popular with weekenders and holiday-makers. Home-smoked fish, home-made *confit*. ROOMS C–E. MEALS A–G. Restaurant shut 16 August–8 September; February holidays; Sunday evening, Monday.

Au Bon Coin, 48 ave Kleber (28.59.12.63). Five rooms. Good cheap restaurant, superb fish. Great value. Live tank for shellfish and trout. ROOMS D. MEALS A–F. Shut 22 December–5 January.

RESTAURANTS

Richelieu (station buffet), place Gare (28.66.52.13). Deservedly famous. Everything refurbished, even table linen. Good wine list. MEALS C–F. Shut Sunday evening.

The best hotel-restaurant around Dunkerque is *La Meunerie* 6km E at Tétegham.

Lille

[MAP 6, page 227]

There are three possible reasons for going to Lille – on business; to see the Musée des Beaux Arts with one of the finest collections of paintings in France; or to eat well. You could also, perhaps, go for the beer.

The vast industrial urban sprawl of Roubaix (*see* page 186) and Tourcoing (*see* page 208) is the greatest economic centre in northern France. The two towns have grown and merged with Lille, making a city of more than a million people. It is still the leading textile city of France, spinning four fifths of the wool spun in France and much of the linen and cotton textiles. Although a lot of nearby coal-mines have become uneconomic and have closed, as have some steel works, Lille has chemical, metal, printing and electronic works, distilleries and famous breweries, and biscuits, chocolate, diesel engines, turbines, tractors and seventy-five million cigarettes are all produced there.

It is a big food-processing centre, too. Its International Trade Fair in April attracts half a million visitors and about the same number arrive in September for its Grande Braderie, a massive, high-powered jumble sale spreading through its streets and squares. Just about anything on earth is sold there.

Lille is at one of the main hubs of the European motorway system, with autoroutes to Paris and the south, Brussels and Germany, and the Channel ports. It is a big railway junction, too. Its industrial zone spreads almost to the Belgian border.

A vast new hospital complex has been built at Lille, and the city has several university and technical colleges, including the world-famous Université des Sciences de Lille at a planned new town, Villeneuve d'Ascq, 8km to the east (*see* page 212).

The Duke of Burgundy lived in Lille, so it became one of the key cities in the wars to decide the ownership of Flanders. It was besieged and nearly starved out eleven times. When Louis XIV was sweeping through Flanders and Germany an arch was erected to him, the impressive Porte de Paris, showing him being crowned by Victory. Then two brilliant generals, the Duke of Marlborough, ancestor of Winston Churchill, and Prince Eugen, the Austrian who had done much to drive the Turks out of Hungary, inflicted a series of heavy defeats on Louis and he had to give up a lot of his conquests in what is now Belgium. But he kept Lille. The monument is next to the modern town hall. When he had taken the city in 1667 Louis had the citadel built by Vauban. It took 2000 men three years to build with sixty million bricks dressed with stone. It is a pentagon and a complete town was built behind its walls. It is surrounded by canals. The main entrance is through a monumental arch, Porte Royale. The army still use the citadel but you can visit on Sunday in summer. Outside there is a zoo and children's playground on the lawns.

The great industrial suburbs hide some lovely old buildings in the old centre. In the early eighteenth century it was called 'Paris of the North'. The seventeenth-century Ancienne Bourse, the old exchange, is a beautiful gem. It was built in the age of the Baroque pictorial stone-cutters and the carved decoration is absolutely superb, with typical Baroque colour. It has twenty-eight houses with an arcaded gallery around a big courtyard – peaceful now but once as frantic as any stock exchange. There is a statue of Napoleon cast from guns captured at Austerlitz. De Gaulle was born in Lille in 1890 and the square is named after him.

Maison de Gilles de la Boé (1636) is richly carved. Rang du Beauregard (1687), in place du Théâtre, is a row of houses carved like a single sculpture. Hospice Comtesse is regarded as one of the finest old buildings in northern France. Founded in 1237, it was rebuilt in the fifteenth century after a fire. The splendid Salle des Malades has wooden vaults and fine arched windows. The kitchen has fine decoration in seventeenth-century Lille and Dutch tiles and the Abbesses' apartments have original furniture. It now houses a museum of local tradition (*Musée Hospice Comtesse*, shut Tuesday). Palais Rihour (1454) was the palace of the Dukes of Burgundy.

Some of the modern buildings put up at the beginning of the century are controversial, to say the least. Comments range from 'especially hideous' to 'merging perfectly with the town centre'. The town hall has a dominating belfry 140 metres high, with sculptures at the bottom of Lille's giants – Phinaert and Lydéric, the most renowned in French Flanders (*see* below). You can climb the tower on Sunday mornings (Easter to end September) for lovely views. The Palais de Justice (1969) is in concrete and glass. The Nouvelle Bourse is neo-Flemish, with a belfry. The Grande Théâtre is in Louis XVI style. These last two were built at the beginning of the century by Louis Cordonnier.

The most interesting church is St Maurice, vast, Gothic, built between the fifteenth and nineteenth centuries with five gables, a lace-work spire and, inside, a fine vaulted ceiling held by a mass of tall columns. The circular Ste Marie-Madeleine church (1675–1713) was being repaired recently – just in time to stop its splendid dome collapsing. Its silver tabernacle door is a masterpiece by the local craftsman Braudoux.

Musée des Beaux Arts (closed Tuesday) is in place République. It is rather bleak but is an artistic treasure house, from its gallery of Primitive paintings to its Impressionist paintings which include Sisley's *La Seine au pont de Suresnes* and Monet's *Thames Scene*. The museum was founded in 1792 when the Lille painter Louis Watteau, nephew of the great Jean-Antoine Watteau, persuaded the local council that the works taken from churches and monasteries in the Revolution should be seen by the people. It was started with four enormous, beautiful altar pieces, two by Rubens, the others by Van Dyck and Jordaens. Apart from works of great masters, including fine drawings by Raphael, not all on show, there are many very good paintings by lesser-known artists of many periods, including a modern *Abstractions* by Sonia Delauney. There are good Goyas, two sculptures by Rodin and a tapestry by Picasso. A wax head was attributed to Raphael, then to Leonardo da Vinci, and was the star of the show. Now it is attributed to a seventeenth-century Fleming, François Duquesnoy, and is therefore no longer a star, though the head is the same.

At No. 9 rue Princesses, where Général de Gaulle was born, there is a museum of documents and photographs of his life, from First World War captain to leader of the Free French in Britain in the Second World War, and President of France.

Lille's giants are brought out on big occasions, especially at Whitsun and the Lille Fête in June. Lydéric and Phinaert date

from 1560 and are 17 metres tall. The legend goes back to
AD600. Phinaert was a brigand who lived in a woodland château.
He attacked the Prince of Dijon and his wife on their way to
England, killing the Prince. The Princess escaped and gave birth
to a son Lydéric, who was brought up by a hermit. When he
grew up, he killed Phinaert in single combat, married the sister
of good King Dagobert, took over Phinaert's forest estates and
founded Lille.

In 1825 they were joined by La Belle Jeanne Mailloté, who
led the women of Lille to drive out armed looters when the men
were away, and later by a fat jolly giant Gambrinus, a good
Fleming who loved beer.

Lille suffered greatly in both world wars, being bombed and
shelled each time. In 1940, 40,000 French troops held off seven
German divisions for three days. The Resistance was strong and
many were shot by the Nazis. The Noble Tour (1459), a trun-
cated tower, surviving from the fifteenth-century ramparts, is
now a memorial to them.

Lille people work hard but play hard, drink a lot of beer in
their brasseries and eat most heartily, in the Flemish way.
During the 'Grande Braderie', a huge, open-air street market
selling secondhand goods of every type, restaurants and cafés
serve, by tradition, mussels and white wine. The theatre has two
well-known companies, there is an excellent philharmonic
orchestra – and a famous football team.

TOURIST INFORMATION Palais Rihour, near place de
Gaulle (20.30.81.00)
MARKET Daily
FESTIVALS April – International Fair; June – fêtes;
September – Floralies; first Sunday in September
Grande Braderie 10 p.m.–1.30 p.m. Monday; New Year
– Winter Fair

HOTELS

Carlton, 3 rue Paris (20.55.24.11). Attractive old classic hotel with classic furnishings. No restaurant. ROOMS E–G. Shut 23 December–1 January.

Treille, 7 place Louise-de-Bettignies (20.55.45.46). Old façade hides new modern hotel. No restaurant. ROOMS D–E.

Strasbourg, 2 rue Jean-Roisin, behind place de Gaulle (20.57.06.46). Recommended cheaper hotel. ROOMS C–E.

RESTAURANTS

Flambard, 79 rue Angleterre (20.51.00.06). One of the truly great restaurants of France. In seventeenth-century house. Painter-chef Robert Bardot is a master. MEALS F–G. Shut August; Sunday evening.

Paris, 52bis rue Esquermoise (20.55.29.41). Slightly less expensive than the three 'greats' of Lille (Flambard, Huitrière, Le Restaurant). A local favourite. MEALS F–G. Shut early August–early September; Sunday evening.

Huitrière, 3 rue Chats Bossus (20.55.43.41). Part of the Lille scene. Art-deco façade of 1930; famous for fish. Book. Very pricey. MEALS F–G. Shut August; Sunday evening.

Féguide, place Gar (20.06.15.50). Railway buffet restaurant. Very popular with locals. Also brasserie. MEALS A (brasserie), C–F. Shut Sunday evening.

Provinciale en Ville, 8 rue Urbanistes (20.06.50.79). Eighteenth-century house. Real Flemish dishes. MEALS D–E. Shut August; Sunday evening, Monday.

Le Club, 16 rue Pas (20.57.01.10). Good cooking, classic and regional dishes – run like a pub. MEALS C–G. Shut 24 December–1 January; August; Sunday (except lunch from September–June).

Lutterbach, 10 rue Faidherbe (20.55.13.74). Good cheap menus. Famous for sauerkraut. MEALS A–F. Shut first week in August.

St Quentin

[MAP 4, page 225]

I have grown to like St Quentin very much, despite the grimy look of many of its buildings, its industry and traffic. Its people are warm and friendly. Go into the most ordinary café and soon a very ordinary citizen or 'la patronne' or the postman will be talking to you.

Fighting went on all around it and in it in the First World War and it was occupied for four years by the Germans, so the very hedges, fields and roads were destroyed, as well as the houses, shops and most old buildings. But when peace came the people cleared a stretch of battlefield and turned it into a beautiful park, which they called Champs Elysées. It has a very pleasant lagoon with a beach beside the river Somme for children's games and watersports. You can hire boats.

The Somme river is canalized and the St Quentin canal links it through the waterway system to the industrialized cities of Nord, Belgium and northern Germany. That was why it was so important in the First World War, when motor transport was primitive. Traditionally a textile town, its industry has switched to chemicals and metalwork. It makes bicycles and cosmetics, too.

The main surviving building is the huge basilica. It was built in the thirteenth century on the site of an earlier church of which the ninth-century crypt remains, containing what is believed to be the fourth-century tomb of St Quentin himself. Its massive belfry can be seen for miles. It looks particularly fine from rue Winston Churchill; though it does not compare with Amiens Cathedral, it is a fine and attractive Gothic building. It was damaged by fire in 1557 when Philippe II of Spain, who was besieging St Quentin, defeated the relieving French army of Constable Montmorency. It was damaged again by shellfire in 1917.

Inside, you are struck by its great width. The nave rises to 35 metres. There is an enormous thirteenth-century choir and five handsome chapels. The delightful glass dates from 1230.

The town hall is extremely ornate Flamboyant Gothic, and very impressive. It was begun in the fourteenth century but its façade is from 1509. It has a pretty eighteenth-century belltower with a thirty-seven bell carillon. Inside, the marriage room has a fine ornamental Renaissance chimney.

Pride of the very good Antoine Lécuyer Museum is a collection of ninety portraits by the pastel painter Quentin de la Tour (1704–88), who was born and died in St Quentin. He painted almost everyone in high society of his time, and had a wonderful talent for half-hidden expressions to catch the personality of his subject. It is surprising that he survived, for although kind and friendly to fellow-artists, it is said that he was almost rude to his important subjects. Perhaps he pleased them by painting them in lovely, smiling, almost theatrical poses. He seems to me to have his tongue in his cheek. Even his self-portrait in the Louvre makes him look happy but slightly vacuous (museum shut Sunday morning, Tuesday).

Another museum, Musée d'Entomologie, 11 rue Canonniers, has 600,000 butterflies and insects, one of the world's biggest collections (shut Sunday, Monday).

One of my favourite buildings is the Grand Hôtel Président in rue Dachery – an old hotel which once looked fit for the scrap heap but has been superbly refurbished and has one of the best restaurants in northern France.

By accident we stayed in St Quentin at Whitsun and ran into Les Fêtes des Bouffons – the Buffoons Fête, traditional since the sixteenth century. It lasts from Friday evening until Monday – a huge street party with half the town in costume, shows, dozens of noisy bands and groups with 'flag-girls'. A great show, but we missed out on the soup, which people were drinking from bowls – sitting, standing, walking. We found out about it too late. On Friday night the Bouffons go round town collecting vegetables from shoppers. At 6 a.m. on Saturday in the market they set up a *marmite* – a huge metal cauldron. Dozens of people wash and peel the veg and make a soup – 'the biggest vegetable soup in the world cooked in the world's biggest cauldron'. You bring your bowl – or buy one for 10F, fill it up, then fill yourself.

TOURIST INFORMATION espace St-Jacques, 14 rue
Sellerie (23.67.05.00).
MARKETS Wednesday, Thursday, Friday, Saturday
FESTIVAL Whitsun – Fêtes des Bouffons

HOTELS

Grand Hotel, Restaurant Président, 6 rue Dachery (23.62.69.77).
Surprising luxury (see text). Superb cooking – light, refined
regional. ROOMS F–G. MEALS F–G. Restaurant shut August; 24
December–2 January; Sunday evening, Monday.
Diamant, 14 place Basilique (23.64.19.19). Very new, modern,
good rooms. Good cheap menu. ROOMS E–F. MEALS B–D.
Paix et Albert I, 3 place 8-Octobre (23.62.77.62). Friendly, pleasant, good value. Restaurant and pizzeria. ROOMS E. MEALS C–F.
Château, Neuville-St-Amand, 3km by rue Gen. Leclerc, then D12
(23.68.41.82). Mansion in park. Only six rooms. Fine classical
cooking. Book. ROOMS E–F. MEALS D–G. Shut 1–19 August;
24–31 December; Saturday; Sunday evening.

RESTAURANT

Pichet, 6 boul. Gambetta (23.62.03.67). Friendly bistro with jolly
evenings. Bourgeois cuisine. Good value. MEALS B–F. Shut Sunday and Monday evenings.

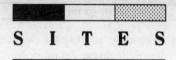
Chantilly

[MAP 3, page 224]

A forest, horse-racing and one of the most attractive châteaux in France – those are the three things for which most of us remember Chantilly.

The château, standing on a little island in a lake formed by the river Nonette, its domed corner turrets, steep roofs and slender chapel spire reflected in the water, is really two buildings – one is the old Petit Château, the other the Grand Château rebuilt in 1880 because the old one had been destroyed in the Revolution.

It is the fifth château built on the site. The first was built by a Roman called Cantilius.

As you approach from the main gate, the sixteenth-century Petit Château is to the left of the chapel. The whole building is now taken over for the remarkable Condé Museum, a splendid collection of paintings, tapestries, furniture and precious stones.

The château was the home in the sixteenth century of the powerful, rich, and brave Anne, Duc de Montmorency, who had the Renaissance château built in 1528. He was confidant, diplomat and military commander to six kings from Louis XII to Charles IX, and for forty years was the most influential man in France after the kings. Made Constable of France, he was called Le Grand Connétable. He owned 130 châteaux and seigneuries (lordships), four large houses in Paris. He went to court surrounded by a guard of 300 knights. Through his five sons and seven daughters he was related or connected with every top family in France. He was taken prisoner at Pavia with his king, François I, ransomed, then defeated the Hapsburg

Château at Chantilly

Emperor Charles V at Susa. He commanded the disastrous attempt to free St Quentin, besieged by the Spaniards (*see* page 64), and became a prisoner again. Commanding the Royal Catholic Army against the Protestants, he was defeated at Dreux and taken prisoner a third time. He was lucky to be rich enough to ransom himself.

In 1563 he drove the English out of Le Havre. He was killed at St Denis in 1567 fighting the Protestants who were commanded by Condé. The Catholic army won the battle and Condé was taken prisoner. Montmorency was wounded in four places but before he died, killed an enemy with the handle of his broken *épée* (sword). His son Henri became a friend and companion-in-arms to Henri IV, le Vert Galant, France's favourite king who loved wine and women equally. The King was constantly falling in love. Aged fifty-four, he stayed at Chantilly with his friend and fell for Montmorency's fifteen-year-old daughter Charlotte. Henri arranged a marriage between Charlotte and a timid and gauche lad Henri de Bourbon-Condé, assuming that her new husband would be no obstacle to Henri's love-affair with his wife. But Bourbon-Condé fled with her on the day after the wedding to Brussels, where they hid under the protection of the King of Spain. Henri IV threatened and even demanded the intervention of the Pope to get the girl back! But he was then murdered by a Jesuit, and the couple returned to Chantilly.

The grandson of le Grand Connétable commanded Catholic armies in the Religious Wars of 1621–30, won victories, and became too popular for Richelieu's liking. Richelieu provoked him into rebellion. He was defeated at Castelnaudry and beheaded. He was the last male Montmorency.

Chantilly was inherited by Charlotte and her husband Bourbon-Condé. Their son, Prince Louis de Condé, was called 'le Grand Condé'. It was he who had the Grand Château rebuilt. He had many great military victories, but fell out with the French royal family, was once imprisoned and then fought for Spain against France. He and Louis XIV became friends. In April 1671 he received King Louis and his Court at Chantilly – 5000 people for a three-day party. Huts were put up in the park to accommodate them, all inns and houses in the surrounding villages were requisitioned. Three meals a day were served at sixty tables. The cooking and an army of cooks and waiters were under the control of Condé's great chef Vatel, 'Controller-general of the Mouth of Monsieur le Prince'. On the first evening, there was not enough roast meat and two tables had none. The next day, the fish due to come from the coast in a convoy of carts had not arrived. Beaten by worry and fatigue, Vatel went to his room and ran a sword through his heart. That is what the French call being 'sérieux' about food!

Condé had had his gardens, park, forest and waterways designed by Le Nôtre, designer of the gardens at Versailles, and they proved to be the forerunner of those at Versailles. Even the rustic 'hamlet' in a corner of the park was copied at Versailles. Marie Antoinette liked to play at being a dairymaid there. When Condé retired to Chantilly he held court there for great writers of the seventeenth century, including Fénelon, Molière, Racine, La Fontaine and Mesdames La Fayette and de Sévigné. His son had the magnificent Grandes Écuries, the great stables, built. Sometimes described as one of the greatest works of monumental architecture of the eighteenth century, they were designed by architect Jean Aubert. They look across to the loveliest of French racecourses. In June, the valuable Prix de Jockey Club for three-year-olds and Le Prix de Diane for three-year-old fillies are run here. The course was built in 1834 when imitating the English was fashionable.

The Chantilly horse-training centre has 2000 hectares of forest, more than 3000 thoroughbred, 80 stables, 100 trainers, 1100 grooms. In the Grandes Écuries is Musée Vivant du Cheval, set up in 1982 – quite the most remarkable horse museum. It has racing horses and ponies and gives shows in its show-ring. There is a super dressage in eighteenth-century costume. (Museum shut Tuesday. In winter open weekends only.) One Prince of Condé said that he would like to be reincarnated as a horse!

In the Revolution, the Grand Château was knocked down to its ground floor, but the stables and Petit Château were spared.

The last of the Condés hanged himself when the 1830 revolution gave the throne to his cousin Louis-Philippe. He left Chantilly to his nephew Duc d'Aumale, a man who had defeated the great Abd El-Kader in Algeria but had been exiled to England for opposing Napoleon III. He left the château and his very mixed collection of treasures to the Institute of France. Experts in any one particular field, such as painting, are not greatly impressed by the heterogeneous collection; to an ordinary visitor the great variety makes the collection very interesting.

Manuscripts were the Duke's great passion, but they cannot all be shown. The most famous treasure, *Très Riches Heures*, painted by the Limbopurg Brothers in the fifteenth century, is too delicate to be shown all the time. But *Heures d'Étienne Chevalier* are shown, and are magnificent. They are forty illuminations painted around 1460 by Jean Fouquet, leading French painter of the fifteenth century, brilliant at miniatures, panel paintings and manuscript illuminators. Two small paintings by Raphael are excellent, and there are several good paintings by Ingres, Delacroix and Géricault. Ceramics, tapestries and the Duke's collection of gems are also in the Grand Château. Alas, the great Rose Diamond is only shown on special occasions under strict security. It was stolen in 1926 and found by accident in an apple, where the thieves had hidden it.

The Petit Château is delightful. In seven large rooms furnished and decorated in seventeenth- and eighteenth-century styles there are wonderful decorations, tapestries, porcelain from Sèvres and Rouen, and almost priceless furniture. The library is extensive and the chapel has fine stained glass and a sixteenth-century altar. (Museum shut Tuesday.)

In the grounds are some wonderful scenes and treasures. Anne de Montmorency set up the Chapelles St Paul et St Jean in 1535 as a memory of the seven churches of Rome which he had visited on pilgrimage to gain Papal indulgence. They were two of seven chapels he built there and he persuaded the Pope to give them the same pilgrimage privileges as those in Rome. Walking round his own estate was easier than walking to Jerusalem or even riding to Rome in a carriage. A third chapel of the original seven, Ste Croix, is by the race-course.

A superb flower garden, La Cabotière, was cultivated in the park by a passionate amateur gardener, a lawyer named Caboud. Maison de Sylvie is a little house where the beautiful Marie-Félicie Orsini, niece of Marie de' Medici, wife of Anne Montmorency's son, and mother of the attractive Charlotte, hid the poet Théophile de Vian when he was wanted by the Paris *parlement* for writing licentious verse. He called her Sylvie and dedicated odes to her. Sylvie fished in the lake alongside.

Two of the most pleasant features of the park are quite different – La Manche, the lake fed by the canalized Nonette river, and the Jardin Anglais with cascades and an Île d'Amour. There is a pathway walk around the park for visitors (shut on Tuesday).

The vast Chantilly Forest, south and east of the château, is mostly fenced in as a state forestry reserve, and used by the privileged for hunting, but several roads pass through. Just north of the village of Coye-la-Forêt on the D118 is a footpath to the pleasant Commelles lagoons. Beside them is Château de la Reine Blanche, a hunting lodge put up in 1826 on the site of a castle built for Blanche of Navarre in 1350 after the death of her husband King Philippe VI of Valois, the man whose succession to the French throne was disputed by Edward III of England, starting the Hundred Years War.

The renowned Chantilly golf course is on the D44 in a lovely woodland setting.

Chantilly's popularity as a country home was partly due to its distance from Paris – 50km. The town is elegant, with bridle paths for horse-riding cut through it.

(See also St Leu-d'Esserent, page 190 – worth visiting while at Chantilly.)

TOURIST INFORMATION 23 ave Mar-Joffre, (44.57.08.58)
FESTIVALS early June – Prix de Jockey Club horse race; second or third Sunday in June – Prix de Diane; June – Concours Complet d'Equitation (horse-riding); first three Saturdays and Sundays of September – Hippiques (show jumping)

HOTELS

Campanile, route Creil N16 N (44.57.39.24). Best cheaper place in a pricey area. Chain hotel. Unexciting. ROOMS D. MEALS A–C.
Relais d'Aumale, Montgrésin, 5km SE (44.54.61.31). In old hunting relais of Duc d'Aumale, recently opened, already draws the horsey set. Elegant bedrooms. Modern cooking. ROOMS F–G. MEALS E–G.

Hostellerie du Lys, at Lys-Chantilly, 7km SW on the N16 and D118 (44.21.26.19).Quiet, attractive, in estate of Lys-Chantilly Forest. ROOMS E–F MEALS E–F. Restaurant shut 22 December–5 January.

RESTAURANTS

Tipperary, 6 ave Mar. Joffre (44.57.00.48). English décor, Irish name, French regional cooking. Best around Chantilly. MEALS D–G.

Relais Coq Chantant, 21 route Creil N16 N (44.57.01.28). Institution of Chantilly. Classy ambience, comfortable, reliable classical cooking. MEALS C–G.

Relais Condé, 47 ave Mar. Joffre (44.57.05.75). Opposite lawns of the race-course. Looks like a private house, but the dining-room was the nave of a chapel! Light classical cooking. MEALS E–G. Shut January; Monday.

Auberge des Étangs, at Coye-la-Forêt 8½km by N16 S, D118 (44.58.60.15). Charming country inn. Nice garden. Good value, good choice. MEALS D–F. Shut 15 January–15 February; Monday evening, Tuesday.

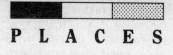

PLACES

ABBEVILLE
[Somme]

Though on the river Somme only 20km from the sea, Abbeville has the bad luck to be on the N1 and it is now an industrial and commercial centre with rather horrific road traffic, despite recent attempts to make through-traffic bypass the town. Once it was a port, shipping wine, wool, salt and dyes to England; it prospered under English rule for 200 years from 1272. The sea started to recede in the eighteenth century.

When I was young, it was a delightful medieval town, the towers of St Vulfran church standing proudly above its old houses. In May 1940 a French division retreating from the German Panzer Divisions tried to make a traditional stand on the Somme as their fathers had done in 1916–17. The French tanks were commanded by Colonel Charles de Gaulle. The 51st Highland Division joined them and made a four-day counter attack, but it failed. The French had managed to hold Abbeville right through the First World War, but they did not have to cope with squadrons of German Stuka dive-bombers. The Luftwaffe and tanks just about wiped out the town in 1940. The Stukas alone destroyed 2000 houses, killed thousands of people and set the whole town alight. The Germans made it one of their most important fighter bases. Later in 1940 the bomber squadron with which I was flying had a private vendetta with the German squadron at Abbeville. On raids over Germany, we would save a small bomb or a few incendiaries, get 'lost' on the way home, and drop them on Abbeville airfield. If we had no bombs, we dropped empty beer bottles with reeds in them. Coming down, they screamed just like a bomb. The Germans must have done a lot of digging looking for unexploded bombs!

After the war, Abbeville was rebuilt on its old street plan, which has not been suitable for modern traffic. However, its industries of textiles, sugar beet and metals have made it prosperous, and it has developed a new personality of action and vitality.

Paris authorities have treated this area very shabbily for new roads, when you think of the amount of lorry and tourist traffic which heads down the N1 to such important places as Rouen, Le Mans, Nantes and beyond. They seem to assume that everyone landing at the Channel ports must want to go through Paris however much that adds to their journey. Going directly south it is very difficult to miss Abbeville.

St Vulfran abbey-church in place Hôtel-de-Ville was started in 1488. Some of it survived the Second World War but for long after it was hidden under huge tarpaulins. Now it is restored and its tall Flamboyant-Gothic façade with two square towers and an open gable is absolutely superb, though the choir built later on a smaller scale looks slightly odd. The façade is rich in fifteenth-century sculptures. The Renaissance carvings of the church doorway were made by local Picardie craftsmen.

Just north of the church is a museum named after Boucher de Perthes (1788–1863), called the Father of Prehistory. His father was Director of Customs for the Somme, based at Abbeville, and he started his archaeological digs in the Somme valley. His finds included stones which he claimed must have been shaped by human hand. At first these were received with scepticism but later were taken as evidence of the antiquity of man.

Driving south on the D901 you see on your left as you leave Abbeville the elegant and beautiful Château Bagatelle, one of the most desirable residences in northern France. It was built in 1752 by an industrialist as a rendezvous with business associations and had only one storey. He added a second storey to live in about fifteen years later and gradually by 1790 it had become a lovely house, in red brick and white stone, surrounded by a truly French park complete with statues. Inside, the house is tastefully furnished with fine panelling. The manufacturer was Abraham Van Robais and you can still see his factory built in 1709, Manufacture des Rames, between chaussée d'Hocquet (D925) and the Somme.

You can take a boat along the canal to St Valery or up the Somme inland to Amiens.

TOURIST INFORMATION 26 place Libération (22.24.27.92)

MARKETS Thursday, last Wednesday in each month

FESTIVAL Early June – Fête-Cavalcade

HOTEL

France, 19 place Pilori (22.24.00.42). Best of a dull lot of hotels. Modern, dull, good value. ROOMS D. MEALS B–E. Restaurant shut 15 December–10 January; Saturday and Sunday lunch in winter.

RESTAURANTS

Escale en Picardie, 15 rue Teinturiers (22.24.21.51). Superbly fresh fish from the Channel. Must book for dinner as fish is bought fresh in late afternoon for number of diners. Popular for lunch. Also has oyster bar for shellfish and white wine. MEALS D–F. Shut 8–13 August; February holidays; Sunday evening, Monday.

Auberge de la Corne, 32 chaussée du Bois (22.24.06.34). More fresh fish but other dishes, too. MEALS B–G. Shut 1–15 August; 1–15 February; Sunday evening, Monday.

AGINCOURT

[*See* Azincourt, page 89]

AILLY-SUR-SOMME

[SOMME]

Small town beside the river on N235 NW from Amiens with a river-bridge and a modern church with a great steep roof like a ship in sail, reaching a stone wall and descending to the ground.

AIRE-SUR-LA-LYS
[Pas-de-Calais]

An interesting, very likeable little old market town beside the old
N43 SE of St Omer, Aire can get very busy on Saturday and
market day (Friday) because it is the shopping town for a wide
area of villages. But the N43 misses most of it and that once-
horrific road has lost most of its heavy lorries and its tourist
traffic hurrying to the A26 motorway. Aire is especially an
agricultural market town, known for geese, ducks and chickens,
confit and *foie gras*.

For a long time it was a fortress town, and has been important for many centuries as four rivers and four canals meet
there. It was mightily prosperous when it was part of the Spanish Netherlands.

Grand'Place is huge, with many narrow but busy streets
running into it, and with eighteenth-century houses around the
edge. There is also a sixteenth-century town hall with a fine
Renaissance balcony from which proclamations have been made
throughout the centuries, an eighteenth-century belfry and a
fifteenth-century church.

St Pierre was a collegiate church, built in Flamboyant style. It
contains a lovely organ chest from 1633 which, sculptured in
oak, is ornamented with statues of musicians. The statue of
Notre-Dame Pannetière used to be the centre for pilgrimages. It
is still carried in procession in early September.

The Captain of the King's Musketeers, D'Artagnan, built a
strong redoubt on the edge of Aire, after Louis XIV had taken
Aire for the French. During the last century a manor house was
built on it – called, inevitably, Château des Trois Mousquetaires.
Now it is one of the most likeable hotels in Pas de Calais, and one
of the best value.

TOURIST INFORMATION town hall in season –

(21.39.07.22)

MARKET Friday

FESTIVALS End April – carnival; early September –
Pilgrimage of Notre-Dame Pannetière; early September
– Fête de l'Andouille (sausage)

HOTEL

Trois Mousquetaires, Château de la Redoute (21.39.01.11). Truly delightful hotel in gabled nineteenth-century château with pointed towers. Lake with ducks and swans. Super regional cooking and charcoal grills. Excellent value. Must book. ROOMS D–F. MEALS B–G. Shut 23 December–18 January; Sunday evening, Monday.

ALBERT
[SOMME]

A modern town since 1918 because it was almost completely destroyed in some of the fiercest fighting in the Battle of the Somme. In 1914 the Germans nearly took the town, but the French infantry and British cavalry drove them to the chalk ridges eastwards. The town was then just behind the French trenches. In 1916 the British 4th Army took it over. In 1915 a German shell had toppled a gilt Virgin from her plinth at the top of the basilica. She did not fall to the ground but hung precariously, head-down. The legend arose that when she fell, the war would end. In March 1918, the Germans took Albert. On 16 April the British artillery knocked down the church tower with gunfire and the Virgin fell. But the British did not take the town until August and the war finished in November. On the town hall, which has a Flemish belfry, is a memorial to the British Machine Gun Corps. The basilica was rebuilt and the Virgin put back. Alas, it is a rather ugly nineteenth-century church. Another Virgin inside the church is from the eleventh century and is still the centre for a pilgrimage on the first and second Sundays in September.

There are many memorials around Albert to mark the dead of those terrible battles. At Thiepval, 4km NE on the D929 and left on the D73 is a memorial to 73,000 British soldiers by the great architect Lutyens who designed New Delhi, Liverpool RC Cathedral and the Cenotaph in Whitehall. The memorial is a sort of brick Arc de Triomphe. On the D929 at La Boiselle a big shell crater (Lochnager Crater) has been preserved, and is owned and maintained by Richard Dunning.

7km N by the D50 is Beaumont Hamel Memorial Park to the Canadians of the Royal Newfoundland Regiment. The river Ancre runs beside it and original trenches have been retained but now they are green with grass – not filthy with mud and blood. A statue of a caribou stands guard.

The Ancre river runs on through the town of Albert, which is an industrial town specializing in metallurgy and aircraft parts. It was called Ancre originally. It was a marquisate and was given in 1610 to Concino Concini, favourite of Marie de' Medici, widow of Henry IV and mother of Louis XIII. Concini, an affected fop, was husband of Marie's childhood friend. He had a great hold over Marie, and because she was Regent of France as her son the king was only nine years old, he had a hold over France itself. He was made Marquis d'Ancre and Marshal of France. When Louis XIII reached sixteen and was technically of age, he ordered the captain of his bodyguard to kill Concini. Then he gave Ancre to his childhood friend Charles d'Albert, Duc de Luynes. The town became Albert.

HOTEL

Grand Hotel de la Paix, 39 rue Victor Hugo (22.75.01.64). Logis de France. ROOMS A–C. MEALS A–C. Shut 1–15 February. Restaurant shut Sunday evening, Monday lunch.

AMBLETEUSE
[PAS-DE-CALAIS]

A very pleasant little seaside resort on a hillside on the Côte d'Opale, the stretch of coast between Calais and Boulogne. It is visited more by French families than British, although it is only 12km N of Boulogne on the D940. It has a big beach of sand, pebbles, rocks and high dunes with the estuary of the little river Slack running through it.

In the seventeenth century it was a naval base, protected by Fort Mahon. Napoleon restored the fort and kept part of his fleet there for the invasion of England. The Germans refortified it in the Second World War against invasion by the Allies. On the road N to Cap Gris Nez a former German blockhouse has become a small museum of the Atlantic Wall – the huge line of concrete defences which the Germans built with slave-labour of people seized from all over Europe to try to foil the Allied invasion.

HOTEL

Bela Brise (21.32.64.84). ROOMS C–F. MEALS B–C.

AMIENS
[*See* Major Towns, page 29]

ARDRES
[PAS-DE-CALAIS]

This attractive, peaceful town, 17km SE of Calais, is built around a green and has crumbling ancient houses with pointed roofs around its triangular cobbled Grand'Place. It is still an important little agricultural centre, and has a factory for making sugar from beet. But it is known mostly for its hotel Grand St Clément, where the Coolen family have cooked so splendidly since 1917. It has a fine fifteenth-century Flamboyant church with a tower dating from 1503.

Ardres has certainly played its part in history. The English took it in 1377 but the French got it back and it became the highly fortified front-line headquarters of the French when the English occupied Calais for 210 years. The marriage of Richard II of England and Isabelle of France took place there in 1396.

Guines was the English front line. The meeting at the Field of the Cloth of Gold between Henry VIII of England and François I of France was held in 1520 between Guines and Ardres beside what is now the D231. The Archduke of Austria took it in 1596 for the Hapsburg Empire but the French got it back two years later. Treaties believed to be world-changing at the time were signed there. Henry and François swore eternal friendship between England and France, then Henry went off and signed an alliance with the Emperor Charles V, France's enemy. During the Wars for Flanders, Louis XIV had Ardres fortified by the great Vauban.

To the north of the town is a lake 2½km long where you can fish, hire a boat, sail or just walk round the edge.

HOTELS

Clément, 91 place Mar. Leclerc (21.82.25.25). I have known it since the early 1950s (see text). Paul Coolen's son François is now at the cooker – a modern chef who keeps old-style regional touches. Very pricey top menu is excellent. ROOMS C–E. MEALS C–G. Shut 15 January–15 February; Monday.

Bonne Auberge, at Brêmes-lès-Ardres on the D231 (21.35.41.09). Real country inn. Simple, very clean rooms. Truly friendly, no frills, informal, old-style cooking. Good-value meals. ROOMS B. MEALS A–E. Shut 15 December–15 January; Sunday evening, Monday in winter.

Relais, boul. Senlecq (21.35.42.00). Logis. ROOMS B–E. MEALS A–D. Shut January 2–6; February; Tuesday.

ARGOULES
[SOMME]

Charming village in the Authie valley with a manor house and with old houses around the village green. The 300-year-old lime tree spreads its branches across the green so thickly that in summer it seems to be under permanent shade. The Auberge du Gros Tilleul is, of course, named after the tree. The village is on the left bank of the Authie river, on the attractive D192. 2km W is the Abbey of Valloires, where in 1346 the bodies of many of the French knights and nobles killed by the English at the Battle of Crécy were taken. It was a Cistercian abbey, built in the twelfth century, but it was burned down and rebuilt in 1741–56. The fine and elegant decorations were the work in 1750 of a

Château d'Argoules

Viennese artist, Baron Pfaff de Pfaffenhoffen, who had fled from Vienna after killing a man in a duel.

From 1817–80 the abbey housed a religious sect called Basiliens who wore a simple blue uniform and devoted their work and time scrupulously to worship. Now the abbey is a children's home but there are guided visits from 1 March to early November. The abbey and church are architecturally simple, the cloisters quite plain, contrasting with Pfaff's refined decoration. The church choir stalls are beautifully carved.

HOTELS

Gros Tilleul, place du Château (22.29.91.00). New owners have improved simple rooms. Pleasant meals. ROOMS C–E. MEALS B–F. Shut end January–early February; Monday.

Coq en Pâté, rue de Valloires (22.29.92.09). Not for snobs. Simple inn run by dynamic lady. Very simple, tiny chalet-like rooms in garden. Good-value meals of country cooking. ROOMS A. MEALS A–C. Shut January, February; Friday.

ARLEUX
[NORD]

Just W of N43 between Douai and Cambrai where the canals du Nord, de la Sensée and the river Sensée meet. SW are Les Étangs de la Sensée – a series of attractive lagoons where many people go to fish, picnic and see waterfowl. Being French they also shoot a lot of waterfowl in season. In France, *la chasse* (hunting) is a religion. Arleux people grow *aulx*, which is the plural of *ail* – garlic. Nearby hamlets include Lécluse (fishing centre), Brunémont (sailing centre with *gîtes* to let [tel. 20.80.91.29], also campsite) and Aubigny-au-Bac (beach with boats and pedalos for hire, sailing, brasserie).

ARMENTIÈRES
[NORD]

Mention Mademoiselle from Armentières to anyone under seventy and they probably won't know what you are talking about. Not many veterans are left from the First World War and 'Tipperary' is one of the few songs still remembered. Mademoiselle, alas, is forgotten.

Armentières is 8km NW of Lille almost on the Belgian frontier. The British cemetery stands silent in the fields on the Lille road out of this modern industrial town where they produce linen and cloth of man-made fibres and brew excellent beer.

The Germans took Armentières in 1914, but the British recaptured it in October 1914 and held it for three and a half years. It was a British base just behind the lines, shelled often by the Germans. The Tommies called Grand'Place 'Eleven o'clock Square' because a shell had stopped the clock on the town hall at that time in 1914. The Germans regained the town in their last offensive in April 1918, and were driven out again by the British in October 1918. Before they left, they mined and destroyed all its main buildings, the old houses of the days of the Spanish occupation and the factories.

The Fête des Nieulles, on the second Sunday in September, celebrates the rebirth of the town between the two world wars. Cakes are thrown from the town hall balcony. At the entrance to the town by pont de Nieppe is one of the most impressive memorials to the French Resistance of the Second World War.

In avenue Salengro is the brewery Brasserie Sébastien Artois, founded in 1650, with a museum of beer (tel. 20.30.89.90). Base des Prés de Hem beside the Lys river is a huge 272-acre park with a 108-acre lake for fishing, sailing and canoeing. There is also canoeing on the river.

MARKET Friday morning
FESTIVAL Second Sunday in September – Fête des
Nieulles (see text)

HOTEL

Albert I, 28 rue Robert Schuman (20.77.31.02). No restaurant. ROOMS C–E.

RESTAURANT

Petite Auberge, 4 boul. Faidherbe (20.77.09.66). Renowned throughout the area for good value. MEALS C–E. Shut Tuesday, Saturday lunch, Sunday evening.

ARRAS
[*See* Major Towns, page 34]

ASCQ
[*See* Villeneuve d'Ascq, page 212]

AUBIGNY-AU-BAC
[*See* Arleux, page 84]

AUDRESSELLES
[Pas-de-Calais]

Very few tourists bother to stop at this seaside village by the D940, S of Cap Gris Nez, but it is a charming little place with low fishermen's cottages and *flobards* (fishing boats) parked in the main street, pulled up on trolleys. Crabs, mussels and other shellfish, even lobster, are sold at the fishermen's cottages and at two little restaurants in the square. The good sand beach has rocks at the end. The small fortified church is from the thirteenth century.

RESTAURANTS

Champenois (21.32.94.68). Superb fish from local boats. Lobster from *viviers*. MEALS A–D. Shut February; sometimes Wednesday.

Chez Mimi (21.32.96.00). More superb fish, little else. Lobsters. MEALS A–D.

AUDRUICQ
[Pas-de-Calais]

Little town among waterways (*wateringues*) and canals NE of
Ardres, 22km NW of St Omer. Centre of a rich agricultural area
specializing in chicory (*endive/chicorée*) and tree nurseries. Its
church contains good eighteenth-century wood sculptures and
there are a few remains of an ancient château – once very
important. Through history, Audruicq was the capital of a canton, fought over for centuries. It was captured by the English in
1352 and changed hands constantly in the Hundred Years War.
The Spanish held it from 1529, the French from 1678.

The eighteenth-century Château de Laurétan was the
attractive house of the lords of Brédenarde. The mansard roof
has a pretty tower at the side.

Audruicq is now a fishing centre, with boat trips on the
canals (tel. 21.82.95.94).

AULT
[Somme]

Family seaside resort between Le Tréport and the Somme
estuary, just off the D940.

HOTEL
Malvina, place Église, Onival (22.60.40.43). By sea. Rooms A–D.
Meals A–C. Open 1 March–31 October. Restaurant shut Friday
evening; Sunday evening except in school holidays.

AUXI-LE-CHÂTEAU
[Pas-de-Calais]

In the Authie valley where the D119 meets the D938 and the
D941, 18km NW of Doullens, and where the river Authie winds
pleasantly through green meadows, with small woods and farm-

ing hamlets. It has a splendid Flamboyant-Gothic church of the sixteenth century – one of the most handsome in the region. Madame de Sévigné loved it when she visited 'this pretty town' in 1684. The vaulting has remarkable carved keystones. One chapel shows angelic musicians.

The old part of the town and the ruins of the castle are in the church quarter.

Auxi makes shoes, basketwork and is famous for enamel. It is a canoeing centre.

MARKET Saturday

AVESNES-SUR-HELPE
[NORD]

This elegant town on the N2, 52km E of Cambrai, is on the left bank of a river called Helpe-Majeure. It still has the remains of Vauban's fortifications. The attractive centre of the town has fine old houses. The town hall in blue stone from Tournai is in classic eighteenth-century style. In the seventeenth century a local Protestant, Jessé de Forest, fled to America and settled in Long Island, New York. Forest Hills was named after him.

From March to September 1918 Field Marshal von Hindenburg, Commander-in-Chief of the German Army, had his General Headquarters in Avesnes, in the *sous-préfecture*. From there he and Ludendorff directed the last German offensive in Flanders, Picardie and on the Marne. Kaiser Wilhelm II reviewed troops in Grand'Place, including Jenny, the elephant whom the Germans had called up to pull down and move trees to consolidate trench positions.

While the weather became cold in Avesnes that September, the war position got very hot for Germans. Hindenburg moved his headquarters to Spa in Belgium, a fashionable place. Grand' Place is now called place du Général Leclerc after the man who led the Free French tank forces so successfully against the Germans after D-Day.

Avesnes produces *boulette d'Avesne* cheese – soft, herb-flavoured, with a red rind and very strong smell and taste. This

Avesnes is not to be confused with Avesnes-le-Comte, an agricultural town in Pas-de-Calais.

TOURIST INFORMATION Syndicat d'Initiative, 41 place
Général-Leclerc (27.57.92.40)
MARKET Friday morning

RESTAURANTS

Crémaillère, 26 place Gén. Leclerc (27.61.02.30). Rustic, friendly; very good cooking of diverse regional and old local dishes. MEALS C–G. Shut 15–30 January; Monday evening, Tuesday.
Auberge du Châtelet, at Les Haies-à-Charmes, 6km N on the N2 (27.61.06.70). Expensive but excellent regional cooking, good vegetables. MEALS C–G. Shut 2–10 January; 15 August–15 September; Sunday evening; Wednesday.

AZINCOURT
[PAS-DE-CALAIS]

Agincourt to you and me – which is why the French don't make a lot of it. Here on 25 October 1415 Henry V of England and his exhausted army, weak with sickness ('We few – we happy few, we band of brothers,' as Shakespeare put it), defeated a French army nearly three times its size, thanks largely to the English and Welsh longbowmen. 'Gentlemen in England this night abed will count themselves accursed they were not here.' The French lost 10,000 knights and 1500 prisoners – one of them the poet brother of the French king, Charles d'Orléans. You can reach the battlefields 15km N of Hesdin (*see* page 149) on the D928. Turn right at Ruisseauville on to the D104 and just before Tramecourt on the left is a great cross marking the mass grave of the French. Further on is a *table d'orientation* showing in English and French the plan of the battle. Arrows mark a footpath from Azincourt village nearby. In the tiny museum in the Mairie at Azincourt is a montage and documents of the battle (tel. 21.04.41.12). In recent years English archery clubs have held a meeting at the battlefield on 25 October.

BAILLEUL
[Nord]

Standing in the Grand'Place it is difficult to believe that Bailleul was almost totally destroyed in the First World War, and very largely destroyed in 1940. Also hard to believe is that all those lovely 'old' Flemish buildings were put up within my lifetime. The gold-brick church, the houses and shops look so old and weathered. Bailleul was in the front line for most of the First World War. The Germans took it in 1914, the British drove them out by mid-October and held it for three and a half years, but German artillery fire destroyed much of it. The Germans took it in 1918 and when the British 25th Division retook the ruins in August 1918 there were only a few dozen buildings left. There is a memorial to the 25th Division at a roundabout and behind Grand'Place are the remains of St Amand church, left in ruins as a war memorial. The church of St Vaast, rebuilt in 1932, has fine coloured windows tracing the town's history. 4km NE along the D23 is the Belgian frontier. Another 19km along the D23 into Belgium is the town of Ieper or Ypres– the 'Wipers' of the British Tommies who fought and died there. It was on the Ypres front, 22 April 1915, that the Germans released poison-gas – the first time that it had been used in war.

From the top of the belfry in Bailleul, which was first built in the twelfth century, you can see far across the countryside to the north and south, and at times you can see Lille to the south-east. The weathercock on the belfry tower is of the fairy Melusine, put there by Flemish tradition to look out for fire or approaching enemies.

The town's giant Gargantua presides over the Carnival Mardi Gras (Shrove Tuesday).

HOTEL

Pomme d'Or, 27 rue d'Ypres (28.49.11.01). Meals (carte only) are good value and cheapish. Rooms B–D. Meals D–E. Shut August. Restaurant shut Sunday and Monday evenings.

BARON
[OISE]

At the twelfth- to thirteenth-century church in this village, 12km E of Senlis, Joan of Arc took communion before going out in 1429 to defeat the English at Senlis. Her headquarters was 5km W of Baron at Châteaufort de Montépilloy, which had been reconstructed around 1400 by Duc Louis d'Orléans, brother of Charles VI. It is now a ruin – part of some farm buildings. Alas, this was the campaign in which she set out to relieve Compiègne which was being attacked by the Burgundians, and she was captured by them, sold to the English, denounced as a heretic by church leaders, and burned.

In Baron's Grand'Rue is the house of a printer, Albéric Magnard, who was killed and burned by the German soldiers on 3 September 1914 for defending himself against them.

BAVAY
[NORD]

Large village N of the Mormal Forest between Valenciennes and Maubeuge. Roman ruins were found there after bombing in May 1940. Standing at the hub of eight roads radiating across Europe, the original Roman town of Bagacum was very important, capital of the Nervii and a big commercial centre until the third century. A huge Roman urban complex with pillars, arcades, shops and baths has been uncovered, with three town walls and, to the west, galleries and a rectangular building. The ruts of chariot wheels can be seen in the Forum. The museum, in a big modern building, has a good collection of bronzes, pottery and glass, and a good audio-visual presentation showing life in the Roman city. (Museum shut Tuesday.)

Bavay is an attractive town, known for confectionery called *chiques de Bavay*, and its local honey.

RESTAURANT
Bagacum, rue d'Audignies (27.66.87.00). Local favourite, despite

décor of stuffed birds. Fresh fish from Boulogne, vegetables from Paris market. In a converted ancient barn. MEALS C–G. Shut 1–22 July; 1–15 January; Sunday evening, Monday.

BEAUREVOIR and BELLICOURT
[AISNE]

Beaurevoir is just east of Le Catelet, which is 19km N of St Quentin on the N44. In the village is a tower of a château where Joan of Arc was held captive by the Count of Luxembourg from August to November 1430, while he bargained to sell her to the English.

Back on the N44, 5km S of Le Catelet, at Bellicourt, there is a cenotaph in white stone commemorating the soldiers of the US 2nd Army Corps who, with the British, breached the 'impenetrable' Hindenburg line here in 1918. St Quentin canal runs underground and the Germans used the long tunnel as part of their defences. A map on the west side of the monument shows the operations of the two US Divisions, and you can see across the plateau to the German trenches. There is a US military cemetery just north at Bony.

BEAUVAIS
[OISE]

I have heard people say that there is little of interest in Beauvais except its cathedral. I disagree. Although it is a commercial town of 60,000 people and had to be largely rebuilt after the German bombardment of June 1940, it is a warm, friendly town, the sort of place to sit outside a café on a fine day and watch people going about their business and pleasure.

The cathedral is magnificent in its new town setting, and in some ways it is a symbol of France. It has survived so many dangers and disasters since it was started in the thirteenth century – and it is still not quite finished! It is a huge Gothic building. In fact, the builders tried to make it *too* big, too high and too light. They built vaults so daring that in 1284 they collapsed, leaving only the apse. When Guillaume de Roye and Aubert d'Aubigny rebuilt it, they gave it extra supporting piers. Their building was completed in 1324. Remarkably, most of the slender panels of stained glass have survived, despite the Hundred Years War, fires, the battle for Flanders and other local differences. The transept was finished early in the sixteenth century. Then the builders got too ambitious again. In the mid-sixteenth century a new tower was built on the piers of the crossing. In 1573, the 153-metre spire collapsed, destroying the tower and badly damaging the transept and its Flamboyant façade. It fell as the procession to celebrate the Ascension was leaving the church. Dangerous masonry was removed by a condemned man in return for his freedom. Repairs cost so much that there was no money left to build the new nave, which has still not been built. The vaulted choir is awesome, reaching 48 metres, nearly as high as the Arc de Triomphe in Paris.

The coloured glass is magnificent, from fourteenth- and sixteenth-century windows, to modern ones by Ingrand and Braque.

There is a remarkable and ornate astronomical clock of the nineteenth century. It shows the movement of tides and planets, and strikes only the hours between noon and 5 p.m. A cock crows at midday.

The church of St Étienne is Romanesque Gothic with a twelfth-century nave and a great high choir in Flamboyant style from the sixteenth century. It has lovely Renaissance windows by Angrand le Prince.

Next to the cathedral is a fairly new tapestry museum with gorgeous tapestries from the fifteenth century to today. Tapestry weaving started in Beauvais by order of Louis XIV, whose Minister Colbert would not spend money on Italian imports of tapestry and lace. The looms were evacuated to Aubusson in 1939, then moved to Paris at the Gobelins.

The art of tapestry design has had a big revival in the past fifty years, mainly due to Jean Lurçat, friend of Cocteau, Picasso and Matisse. He died in the 1960s.

Beauvais' local heroine is Jeanne Hachette, who roused the

Detail from stained-glass window, St Étienne

people to fierce defence when Charles le Téméraire (Charles the Bold) of Burgundy was attacking the city with 80,000 men in 1472. Seeing an enemy soldier climbing over the ramparts with a banner, this girl grabbed his banner, chopped it up with a hatchet and threw it in the moat, which roused the people to resist until help came.

A fête to celebrate her courage is held at the end of June.

The local villain is the Bishop of Beauvais who helped the English and Burgundians against the French and was one of the churchmen who found Joan of Arc guilty of heresy.

TOURIST INFORMATION Office de Tourisme, rue St Pierre (44.45.25.26)

MARKETS Wednesday, Saturday

FESTIVAL Late June – Fête Jeanne Hachette

HOTEL

Palais, 9 rue St Nicolas (44.45.12.58). Cheerful, clean, comfortable. No restaurant. Near cathedral. ROOMS C–D.

RESTAURANTS

Crémaillère, 1 rue Gui-Patin (44.45.03.13). Old favourite of my readers. MEALS C–G. Shut Wednesday.
La Côtelette, 8 rue Jacobins (44.45.04.42). Very good classical cooking. Quite pricey. MEALS E–G. Shut Sunday evening, Monday.

BERCK PLAGE
[PAS-DE-CALAIS]

In 1861, when this beach resort was already the haunt of artists such as Manet and Boudin, a widow named Madame Brillard, who had lost not only her husband but also four children, took in some very sick children for a recuperative holiday; the very iodized climate proved so good for them that the local medical authorities decided to set up a centre for treating bone disorders. In 1869 the Empress Eugénie, wife of Napoleon III, opened the hospital which is still there. There are now 3000 beds for people taking treatment.

But Berck is not just a place to seek medical help. It has a 12km beach of fine sand and is unsophisticated but lively, so it is popular with French families.

Berck was settled in the ninth century by Norsemen. They had come to loot and burn but their ships were wrecked, so they could not go home.

Berck has rather too many brash amusement arcades and suchlike. But it also has a casino, as well as the Agora sports complex beside the beach, with a covered swimming-pool and a skating rink. The Bagatelle Amusement Park (*see* Merlimont, page 166) is 5km N.

Le Phare (the lighthouse), rebuilt after the Second World War, is 40 metres high with 200 steps (open afternoons). Berck has good-value restaurants. Horse-races in mid-August.

TOURIST INFORMATION 5 ave Francis Tattegrain
(21.09.50.00)
MARKETS Wednesday, Sunday morning

HOTELS

Marquenterre, 31 ave Francis Tattregrain (21.09.12.13). Formerly the 'Trou Normand'. Attractive bourgeois mansion. Garden. ROOMS C–D. MEALS A–D. Shut 18 December–12 January; Sunday evening; Friday in winter.

Homard Bleu, 48 place Entonnoir (21.09.04.65). Good fish. Comfortable restaurant. ROOMS C–D. MEALS A–G. Shut holidays of November, February; Sunday evening and Monday in winter.

RESTAURANT

Auberge du Bois, 149 ave Quettier (21.09.03.43). Good value. Known for fish soup. MEALS C–F. Shut 3 January–1 February; Monday.

BERGUES
[NORD]

A charming Flemish town only 8km from Dunkerque, still snug behind the fortifications erected by Vauban for Louis XIV. Despite wars and the Revolution, it still has its towers, some dating from the Middle Ages, its walls, canals (which acted as moats) and four gateways – Cassel, Hondschoote, Dunkerque and Bierne. The warm yellow-ochre bricks look magnificent reflected in the moats. Although it was badly damaged in 1940, it keeps its ancient character with winding streets, large squares and now-silent quays by the Colme river.

Vauban's complicated system of canals and defences, called Couronne d'Hondschoote, is still impressive. The French used the fortifications as a defence in 1940 and the Germans tried to breach them by dive-bombing with Stukas. The lagoons which are part of the system are now used for pleasure. You can take a pedalo or rowing-boat around them.

Of the medieval abbey of St Winoc two towers remain, one

square and massive, the other, Tour Pointu, more delicate. Pointu was rebuilt in 1815 after destruction in the Revolution. The beautiful belfry, a square tower in sand-coloured brick 54 metres high, with an octagonal bell tower, was actually rebuilt since the Second World War – a faithful copy of the original. The Germans deliberately blew it up before they were thrown out by the Canadians in 1944. It has a carillon of fifty bells which are played at 11 a.m. on Monday and 5 p.m. on Saturday.

Bergues was ceded to France under the Treaty of Aix-la-Chapelle in 1667. It was a wool town and was so prosperous once that it rivalled Dunkerque. Mont-de-Piété, built in 1629, was a symbol of its commercial activity. Mont-de-Piété is a pawnshop, and this was the first one in Flanders, used in those days to find money to fund commercial enterprises. It was built by Wenceslas Coebergher, a man of many talents. He was a painter, engineer, economist and architect. In Flanders he drained marshes. Later Mont-de-Piété became an almshouse.

Inside Mont-de-Piété is a museum with some fine Flemish and French paintings. They include one of many versions of the *Hurdy-Gurdy Player* by La Tour. This one has a small dog in it. *Fog – The Dunes at Poulignac* is notable. It is by Maxime Mauffra, who later fell under the spell of Gauguin. There are works of Van Dyck, Brueghel the Elder and Rubens.

You can go round Bergues in a little street-train.

TOURIST INFORMATION Town hall (Easter–15 September – 28.68.60.44)

MARKET Monday

FESTIVAL Palm Sunday – Agricultural Fair

HOTEL

Tonnelier, 4 rue du Mont-de-Piété (28.68.70.05). In a cooper's house of 1679. Owned by same family for ninety years. Regional bourgeois cooking. ROOMS B–D. MEALS A–F. Shut 15 August–early September; 1–22 January; Friday.

RESTAURANT

Cornet d'Or, 36 rue Espagnole (28.68.66.27). In a classified house from the Spanish occupation. Modern cooking, rather pricey. MEALS E–G. Shut 15 June–early July; Sunday evening, Monday.

BERNAY-EN-PONTHIEU
[SOMME]

Hamlet on the W edge of Crécy Forest where the river Maye forms little lakes. It is on the N1, and still has its old post house and auberge mentioned by Victor Hugo in 1837 as being placed exactly at the spot where passengers on the coach from Paris were hungry for lunch, and those from Calais were hungry for dinner. The stables are still there in the courtyard. 2km W is Château d'Arry, a Louis XV manor built in 1761 in pink brick and white stone on a hillside overlooking the Maye.

BÉTHUNE
[PAS-DE-CALAIS]

Just off the A26 motorway NW of Arras, Béthune long prospered as the centre of a coal-mining area, despite being wiped out in 1918. Its position as a port on the Aire canal, connected with waterways leading to Lille NE and Gravelines and Dunkerque NW, ensured its importance. It is still an important rail town. With the closing of mines in northern France over recent years, it has had to change to new industries and has built up a modern industrial zone with very varied products, and has prepared for years for the 1992 open markets. It is a centre still for the market gardens around it.

Houses of the seventeenth and eighteenth centuries are in the quarter of rue de la Déliverance. But the joy of Béthune is its Grand'Place. It was virtually wiped out in the Second World War, but rebuilt most attractively in Flemish style. The massive fourteenth-century belfry, 40 metres high, was rebuilt, too – a strong, restrained tower in sandstone. The sixteenth-century church of St Vaast to the north was also rebuilt from rubble; only its belfry had survived. The houses in Grand'Place really seem to be jostling each other to show their faces in the square.

Béthune was a British headquarters town from 1915–18. Before that it had been held by the Indian Corps. The Germans managed to take only part of it in 1918. The British held the rest. The town is twinned with the old port of Hastings in East Sussex.

The canal and old port have found new life as a watersports and leisure centre, with a marina.

TOURIST INFORMATION 34 Grand'Place (21.68.26.29)
MARKETS Monday, Friday

HOTELS

Vieux Beffroi, 48 Grand'Place (21.68.15.00). Comfortable, middle-priced, in town centre. ROOMS B–D. MEALS B–E.
Chartreuse du Val St-Esprit, Gosnay, 5km SW by N41, D181 (21.62.80.00). Charming hotel in eighteenth-century '*gentilhommerie*'. Meals pricey. ROOMS E–F. MEALS C–G.

RESTAURANT

Marc Meurin, 15 place République (21.68.88.88). Inventive cuisine. MEALS C–G. Shut August; Sunday evening, Monday.

BLÉRANCOURT
[AISNE]

In 1917, Anne Morgan arrived here with an American volunteer unit to help the villagers nearby who had been turned out of their homes by fierce fighting in which areas were changing hands constantly. The unit brought ambulances, clothing, blankets, food, emergency kitchens, nurses and helpers. Young American girls (mostly students) were driving rickety Model T Ford ambulances over pot-holes and tracks to save lives. Their headquarters was in the remains of a seventeenth-century château abandoned since the Revolution. It is E of Compiègne through the Laigue Forest.

Anne Morgan was the sister of the American banker J. Pierpont Morgan. When the fighting ceased, she and another rich American girl from the unit, Ann Murray Dike, helped the destitute villagers to rebuild their lives. They were also the driving force behind the restoration of the château as the national museum of Franco-American cooperation.

The château was built in 1612 by the son of a Paris furrier who had risen to power at court, Salomon de Brosse, on the site of an ancient château of the Ducs de Gesvres. It was designed by Mansard, in the style of Luxembourg Palace in Paris. You enter from what was the back drive on to the garden. It looks even more impressive from the front, where the grounds run down to a tiny river.

The museum is devoted mostly to the American War of Independence and the French part in it, and to US forces in the First World War. You can see one of those Model T ambulances and wonder how the students drove them, and how the wounded survived. This one was driven by a young American volunteer, Edward Seccombe of Derby, Connecticut, who bought it after the First World War, had it restored at his own expense, and shipped it to the château. Significantly, there is little in the museum about Franco-American cooperation after the Second World War.

A pavilion lodge by the back gate where you enter the château is a charming hotel, opposite a huge village green. There is a lovely drive along route Eugénie through Laigue Forest to Compiègne.

HOTEL

Hostellerie Griffon (23.39.60.11). Comfortable, charming little hotel in château lodge. Open garden pavilion for summer meals. Good value. ROOMS E. Meals C–F. Shut 23–30 December; Sunday evening, Monday.

BLÉRIOT PLAGE
[PAS-DE-CALAIS]

Only 3km from Calais, its beach of sand and dunes continues past Sangatte (where the Chunnel starts), 1km to Cap Blanc Nez. On 25 July 1909, Louis Blériot took off from the beach and flew to a field near Dover – the first Channel air crossing in a heavier-than-air craft. He took a half hour. There is a monument near the D940. At Cap Blanc Nez is a monument to Latham (1883–

1912), an airman who tried to beat Blériot's time and came down in the sea. The incentive for the flight was £1000 (a large sum then) offered by the London *Daily Mail*.

Blériot Plage was called Les Barraques until 1936. By the beach is a new VVF (Village-Vacances-Famille) – like a much cheaper Club Mediterranée or simpler Butlin's. Holiday bungalows are among the dunes.

HOTEL

Dunes (21.34.54.30). Popular with Calais people for meals. Rooms B–D. Meals B–F. Shut Sunday evening; Monday in winter.

BONDUES
[NORD]

12km N of Lille. Nearby is Château de Vert Bois, a charming eighteenth-century manor surrounded by a moat. It contains a wonderful collection of ceramics, including old Delft, and pieces by great artists (Renoir, Picasso, Dufy, Rouault, Chagall) as well as a beautiful collection of rare stones. It is open only on Sunday afternoon (shut 15 July to 15 August). In the attached farm, Le Septentrion, exhibitions are held, mostly of modern painters and sculptors. There is also a restaurant, an antique shop and a craft boutique.

BORAN-SUR-OISE
[OISE]

Village SW of Chantilly on the river, popular on fine weekends with bathers and sunbathers, and with fishermen in wetter weather. It is on the right bank, with a bridge joining it to a beach on the opposite bank, with views of the Carnelle Forest heights. The thirteenth- to fifteenth-century church has a Gothic clocktower with fourteenth- to fifteenth-century statues.

6km SW, just over the department border in Val de l'Oise, is the old fortified town of Beaumont-sur-Oise and Château de Nointel with a vast park. In the seventeenth century its gardens were some of the finest in France. Excellent steps and statues remain.

4km SE of Boran is Abbaye de Royaumont (Val de l'Oise), a most interesting medieval abbey.

BOULOGNE
[See Major Towns, page 38]

BRAY DUNES
[Nord]

A little resort on the Belgian frontier, very near to the fashionable Belgian resort of De Panne. Bray is on the huge sand beach stretching from Malo-les-Bains at Dunkerque into Belgium – the beach from which the Dunkerque evacuation took place in 1940 (*see* Dunkerque, page 54). On the promenade is a memorial to the 12th French Infantry Division who held off the Germans here until 4 June 1940, 'Pour l'honneur'. Rather than capitulate, though hopelessly outnumbered, they fought on to help the British and French soldiers to get away in ships.

BRAY-SUR-SOMME
[Somme]

On the Somme, W of Péronne, this is a favourite freshwater fishing centre for the river, the canal and lagoons. It was once an important river-port. On a bend in the river, Belvédère de Vaux gives a splendid view of the river and its many green islets.

HOTEL
Étangs du Levant, rue Moulins (22.76.00.90). Beside a lagoon. Rooms B–C. Meals A–D. Shut part of January, February; Tuesday except summer.

BRIMEUX
[Pas-de-Calais]

In the Canche valley, 8km SE of Montreuil, with fishing in a large lagoon and the river. Important in Gallo-Roman days, it has also a sixteenth-century church with a Flamboyant choir and a strange belltower.

CALAIS
[*See* Major Towns, page 47]

CAMBRAI
[Nord]

Any town which has been through the trials of Cambrai and comes out reasonably prosperously is sure to be happy. It is close to the fairly new A26 motorway, and the A2, which has improved its commercial communications enormously. The horrors of all those heavy vehicles on the N43 are blessedly already disappearing.

The flat plains around are not pretty, but they are rich, and cereals and sugar beet are grown there, as well as the cotton made in Cambria into fine lawn (cambric) used for expensive handkerchiefs and lingerie. Chicory (*endive/chicorée*) is another traditional crop.

Cambrai was part of Spanish Flanders until the seventeenth century, and despite its terrible war damage in the Second World War, it still has a rare Maison Espagnole of carved wood (1595), a phoenix reborn after fire in 1917, lovely seventeenth-to eighteenth-century houses, and Porte Notre-Dame, the old gateway with diamond-shaped stones.

The Cathedral of Notre-Dame was built in the eighteenth century, frequently restored, but always in neo-classical style. Inside is a monument to Fénelon by David d'Angers. Fénelon, the great writer-priest, upset Louis XIV by publishing his story *Télémaque*, which the King believed to be a satire of his court. The King had made him Bishop of Cambrai, but he was then forbidden to travel outside his diocese. He died in Cambrai aged sixty-four after his carriage crashed in 1715.

There is a statue of Fénelon (1947) in the square, from where you can also see the Chapelle du Grand Séminaire, an old Jesuit chapel built in seventeenth-century Baroque style popular in Flanders. It contains a treasury of religious art from the Middle Ages to the nineteenth century. The church of St Géry nearby has a huge dramatic painting of the *Entombment* by

Rubens. More interesting to tourists is the belfry of the fifteenth-century St Martin church, 70 metres high, with two mechanical figures called Martin and Martine who hammer a bell every hour.

Another very unusual picture of the *Entombment* is in the Musée Municipal, 15 rue de l'Épée (shut Tuesday). This one is by a Flemish painter, Hendrik de Clerck. The museum has good Dutch, Flemish and French paintings, including works by Rubens, Ingres and Boudin, modern works of Utrillo, and sculptures of Rodin and Bourdelle. Some drawings by Matisse and Dufy are shown only on special occasions for fear of deterioration. There are also works of the eccentric rebellious artist Maurice de Vlaminck, who was a racing cyclist, then a violinist before he took to painting.

The destruction of Cambrai during both world wars was particularly bad. The town was not only the scene of one of the most important battles of the First World War, from 20 November to 7 December 1917, but also the great German defence wall of blockhouses, barbed wire, trenches, artillery and machine gun posts called the Hindenburg line ran through the very centre of it. Furthermore, the British used mass tank forces in battle for the first time. Having invented the war tank, the British had not had much faith in it, and had used it in small numbers without much success on only two occasions. At Cambrai they had 476 tanks, brought in secret from the little port of Richborough in Kent on a train ferry under tarpaulin, then on trains from Calais. They were hidden in ruined villages and a wood behind the lines, and moved up overnight, the sound of their engines drowned by low-flying aircraft.

The British had to cross heavily defended rivers and canals, but so successful were the tanks that within four hours the Hindenburg line was in British hands, except for one village. Alas, the British Divisional Commanders, especially the commander of the 51st Highland Division, mistrusted tanks and kept their infantry too far behind them, so that the Germans were able to regroup and take back the British gains; but warfare was changed that day. The Tank Corps Staff Officer General J. F. C. Fuller wrote a book after the war on tank warfare which did not impress his own Army Commanders. He advocated mobile warfare with lightning attacks by armoured units. The book *did* impress de Gaulle, who called Fuller one of the greatest military brains in Europe. And it impressed Hitler and his commanders so much that they 'invented' the blitzkreig. One of the tank commanders at Cambrai, wounded and given the Military Cross, was Major Clement Attlee – Labour Prime Minister of Britain after the Second World War.

French and Burgundians quarrelled over Cambrai for centuries. It was taken by Louis XIV in 1677, captured by Wellington in 1815, the Prussians in 1870, German General von Kluck in August 1914 and occupied by the Germans from May 1940 to September 1944.

The string of little lakes and the canal Sensée northward (*see* Arleux, page 84) are popular for picnics, fishing and watersports.

TOURIST INFORMATION 48 rue Noyon (27.78.26.90)

MARKET Daily except Monday

FESTIVALS First Sunday in July – Brocant (second-hand sale); early September – Kermesse (festival)

HOTELS

Château Motte Fénelon, allée Saint-Roch (27.83.61.38). Small fin-de-siècle château with bungalows in its park. The château was built by a laundryman who used the land originally for drying-fields, made a fortune, married into Cambrai Society and built the château. There are two upstairs dining-rooms and a restaurant, Les Douves, in cellars. Well-furnished rooms. ROOMS E–G. MEALS D–F. Restaurant shut Sunday evening.

Mouton Blanc, 33 rue d'Alsace-Lorraine (27.81.30.16). Old Flemish style; comfortable, pretty bedrooms. Old-style family cooking (pot-au-feu, boeuf bourguignon). Good value. Near station. ROOMS C–E. MEALS B–F. Restaurant shut Sunday evening, Monday.

RESTAURANT

Escargot, 10 rue Gén. de Gaulle (27.81.24.54). Excellent grills. The place to try the famous local sausage (*andouillette de Cambrai*). Real charcoal grill. MEALS A–F. Shut 20 August–9 September; Monday.

LA CAPELLE-EN-THIÉRACHE
[AISNE]

16km S of Avesnes-sur-Helpe. This little town played its part in history on 7 November 1918, when a German delegation led by General Von Winterfeldt and the German Secretary of State, Erzberger, who were making for Compiègne to arrange an armistice, were received by the French town Commandant after passing through the advance French front line at Haudroy, 3km NE. They were led to Ville Pasques (17 rue de l'Armistice) where they left their Mercedes to get into French cars with nostalgic names – Panhard, De Dion, Delaunay and a Renault. Then they drove on to near St Quentin to meet the Commandant of the French 1st Army. The Armistice was signed on 11 November. 3km along the D285, beside the road where the Germans passed through French lines, is Pierre d'Haudroy, the Armistice monument.

CASSEL
[NORD]

On the D916, 29km S of Dunkerque, Cassel is built on the slopes of Mont Cassel, which stands 175 metres above the Flanders plains. Not surprisingly, it has been fortified and fought over through the centuries. On clear days you can see the sea 30km away. The Romans made it the hub of seven roads. Normans, Flemish, Spanish, French, British and Germans have fought to take it and hold it.

A hundred years ago there were twenty-nine windmills on the slope. Now they are represented by one, reconstructed from a sixteenth-century mill which burned down in 1911. It shares place of honour with a huge equestrian statue of a late honorary citizen, Marshal Foch, who made his headquarters here from October 1914 until June 1915 during the Battle of Flanders. He stayed in the eighteenth-century Hôtel de Schoebeque, which is still a hotel. It was visited by King George V of England, the Prince of Wales (later Duke of Windsor), King Albert I of the

Belgians and Field Marshal Douglas Haig. Foch's statue is set in a garden where a feudal château once stood.

In 1940 the retreating British forces on their way to Dunkerque fought street by street through Cassel against the German Panzer Divisions; 2000 were killed and 1000 taken prisoner.

There is a museum in Foch's old office opposite the town hall in rue Maréchal Foch. Here Foch planned the final Allied drive which ended the war in 1918. It is open on Sunday afternoon in summer or by request at the town hall – a new one built after the old one from 1634 was flattened by the Luftwaffe in 1940.

Today, Cassel is a charming town with narrow sloping streets, some cobbled, and flights of steps. Grand'Place, now named Place Général de Gaulle, is elegant and attractive.

Cassel is known for fêtes and carnivals, featuring its giants Reuze Papa and Reuze Maman.

TOURIST INFORMATION Town hall, 15 rue Notre-Dame
(28.42.40.19)
MARKET Thursday morning
FESTIVALS First Sunday in March – procession of the
giant Reuze Papa; Easter Monday – Carnival of the
Giants; third Sunday in June – Festival of the Patron
Saint (Ducasse)

HOTELS

Schoebeque, 32 rue Mar. Foch (28.42.42.67). See text. Good restaurant. ROOMS C–E. MEALS C–F. Shut February; Monday.

RESTAURANT

Sauvage, Grand'Place (28.42.40.88). In sixteenth-century house where Napoleon, King George V and US President Wilson have slept. Panoramic views over Flanders. Superb regional dishes. Home-made bread and chocolates, 600 different wines. MEALS C (rustic, good value), F, G. Shut Sunday and Tuesday evening, Wednesday.

LE CATEAU-CAMBRÉSIS
[NORD]

The artist Henri Matisse was born in 1869 in this charming town on the river Selle, son of a grain merchant. The importance of Le Cateau is still that it is on the borders of the grain-growing country of Cambrai and the rich pastures of Avesnes.

The statue in Grand'Place is not of Matisse, who died in 1954, but of Adolphe Mortier, son of a local silk merchant. This enormously strong soldier performed wonders for Napoleon in Germany, Russia and Spain, and was made a Marshal of France. He was later a favourite of King Louis-Philippe and died saving the King's life by throwing his great bulk between him and a bomb intended to assassinate him.

Le Cateau was Wellington's headquarters in 1815.

Grand'Place is named after the writer Anatole France and has a seventeenth-century town hall with a very elegant belfry from 1705.

Palais Fénelon, in rue Charles-Seyeoux, was the palace of the Archbishops of Cambrai, of whom the writer Fénelon was one. It has classical lines and a classical French garden bordered by the river Selle. Inside the palace is Cateau's tribute to Matisse, a museum transferred here in 1970 from the town hall and called after him. He gave the town a number of his works – sculptures, paintings, a tapestry and engravings. The family gave other works and items.

Matisse was one of the greatest and also most influential artists of this century. He was one of the original Fauvist painters, influencing Vlaminck, Dufy, Rouault and others. He used bold, brilliant primary colours in two-dimensional patterns. His line-drawing was magnificent. Many of his works here are from his early days, including nudes from his days at Bouguereau Academy in Paris. The self-portrait was painted in Nice in 1918. The 1946 Gobelins tapestry *The Lute* is excellent.

His family lived in the nearby village of Bohain but he was born at his grandparents' house at 45 rue République in Le Cateau. In a nursery school in rue General Morland (now called École Matisse) is the last stained-glass window he designed, just after he designed the famous windows in the chapel at Vence in Provence.

In Le Cateau museum, one floor is given to works of Auguste Herbin (1882–1952), another local artist, who became a cubist then abstract painter.

TOURIST INFORMATION Palais Fénelon, place Cdt E. Richez (27.84.13.15)

MARKETS Tuesday, Thursday, Saturday morning

HOTEL

Relais Fénelon, 21 rue Mar. Mortier (27.84.25.80). Only three rooms. Garden. ROOMS C. MEALS C–E. Shut 6–27 August. Restaurant shut Sunday evening, Monday.

CAYEUX-SUR-MER
[SOMME]

Little seaside resort which can get windy, on a coast road, the D102, round Cap le Hourdel on the southern tip of the Somme estuary. It has a huge, long beach of sand and pebbles with dunes and a 1600-metre promenade. Just back from the beach is a village called Brighton-les-Pins. Southward towards Ault are the Hable d'Ault lagoons. There are many caravans and untidy holiday chalets on the coast road.

At le Hourdel is a tiny fishing port also used by pleasure boats (especially when it blows) and a lighthouse (visits 1 April to 30 September). Pebbles are collected from this stretch as far as Ault for grinding to make emery and filters. Cayeux has pedalos for hire, a sailing club and is good for sea fishing.

HOTELS

Côte d'Opale, 158 rue Mar. Foch (22.26.76.76). Simple rooms. Famous fish soup. ROOMS A–B. MEALS A–E. Shut 15 November–15 December; Tuesday.

Parc aux Huîtres, le Hourdel (22.26.61.20). Good fish, especially *marmite du pêcheur*. Beside sea. Enclosed glass terrace. ROOMS C–E. MEALS B–E. Shut 15 December–15 January; Tuesday evening, Wednesday except mid-summer.

CHAMBLY
[OISE]

Known for its folklorique fête 'Bois Hourdy' with bonfires and cavalcade on the Sunday following Shrove Tuesday (Mardi Gras), which commemorates King Louis IX (St Louis) who founded the church in the thirteenth century. Louis (1215–70) was the deeply religious king who landed 40,000 men in Egypt on a Crusade, was defeated by the Saracens, taken prisoner and ransomed. He set off again, got to Tunis and died of plague. He did improve the French Courts of Justice, and set up provincial *parlements*, both designed to take away the excessive rights of local lords over the people.

The N1 just misses Chambly, W of Chantilly.

CHÂTEAU-THIERRY
[AISNE]

Though it has been of great historical significance in wars, this ancient town, 96km NE of Paris, where two arms of the river Marne meet, is important to most Frenchmen as the birthplace of La Fontaine, poet of fables. No other country holds its writers and artists in such esteem as France does.

Jean de la Fontaine was born here on 8 July 1621, son of a civil servant who was Master of Waterways and Forests and Captain of the Hunt. Young La Fontaine skipped school classes to go for walks, then, after hearing religious lectures, decided on the spot to become a priest. He entered a religious order but both he and his teachers decided he was not cut out to be a celibate. He went back to Château-Thierry in 1644 and hardly left it for thirteen years. His father bequeathed him the civil service job, and married him to a police-lieutenant's daughter, but he neglected both to feast at his friends' houses and woo their women. He was frivolous, dissipated but charming and they all liked him. Then he heard an officer repeating an ode by Malherbe and decided that *he* was a poet, too. He studied the old writers and wrote his own verse. He rapidly became successful

Well outside La Fontaine's house

and at thirty-six was made poet to Nicolas Fouquet, Louis XIV's finance minister. When the ambitious Fouquet was imprisoned for having his hand in the Royal purse, La Fontaine stayed in Paris, became a literary lion of high society, and died there in 1695. His *Stories and Fables* in verse are lively and original. When I was young, every child learning French, whether French or foreign, learned by heart the fables of the cock and the fox, the wolf and the lamb. He was a brilliant writer and one of the first poets to love the countryside and nature, and not regard it as wild and barbaric, as was fashionable in Louis XIV's day.

The sixteenth-century La Fontaine house is now a museum, with busts, drawings, gravures and editions of his work. It is a dreary house and a dull museum, unworthy of such a lively, fun-loving poet, but it does have a section devoted to fables through the centuries (shut Tuesday).

The ruins of the great château itself stand above the town,

with views over the old ramparts and Marne valley. It was named after the Mérovingien King Thierry IV, shut up here by Charles Martel, who became effective ruler of all the Franks. Martel was the man who drove the Moors out of France after defeating them at Poitiers. Thierry died in the castle in AD737. Its remains now stand in a pleasant park.

Two ancient gates and a tower remain from the old ramparts. On one gate, Porte St Pierre, is an inscription recalling that in 1429 Joan of Arc left the town by this way when she had delivered it from the English.

Tour Balhan is a fifteenth-century Gothic belfry with a sixteenth-century campanile.

In February 1814 Napoleon defeated the Russian-Prussian army of Blücher under the walls of Château-Thierry. On 3 September 1914, the Germans took the town and pillaged it. On 9 September the Corps of the British Expeditionary Force took it back and made their first crossing of the Marne. It remained in Allied hands until 1 June 1918, when the Germans took it and held the 'Château-Thierry pocket'. On 21 July it was liberated by the French, aided by the Americans in their first major offensive. It had been heavily looted and sacked by the Germans. The repairs to the bridges and town had not been long completed when the Germans devastated it again with bombing in 1940.

Take the N3 W from the town and a little road takes you up Côte 204, the hill which the Americans took after very fierce fighting. Here is an enormous American memorial of a double colonnade above a terrace. On the west are figures representing France and America, on the east a huge eagle perched over a map of the area where the Americans fought.

Go back on the main road and cross it on to the little D9 to Belleau, 8km away, where the Americans gained another famous victory in 1918. In the centre of Belleau Wood nearby is a memorial to the 4th US Marine Brigade who captured this area on 25 June 1918, after terrible fighting. Among trees are the guns they captured. In the street of Belleau are the château stables where they were billeted afterwards and a chapel with an imposing tower in a cemetery where 2288 men are buried. Nearby is a cemetery where 8625 Germans are buried.

Champagne is made in thirteenth-century caves in Château-

Thierry (Champagne Pannier – tel. 23.69.13.10. Tours and tastings daily except Sunday).

TOURIST INFORMATION 12 place Hôtel-de-Ville,
Château-Thierry (23.83.10.14)

MARKETS Tuesday, Friday

FESTIVAL Three days in late June – Carnivale et Fête La Fontaine

HOTEL

Île de France, 2km on D1 route Soissons (23.69.10.12). Friendly, good hotel. Good value. ROOMS C–E. MEALS B–F. Shut 23–30 December.

RESTAURANT

Auberge Jean de la Fontaine, 10 rue Filoirs (23.83.63.89). Recent new owner and chef, becoming popular around the region. MEALS E–G. Shut 1–21 August; 2–22 January; Sunday evening, Monday.

COMINES
[NORD]

This industrial town, 20km NW of Lille, is French on the right bank of the river Lys, and Belgian on the left! It must have had trouble before the EC was formed.

Philippe de Commynes, French statesman and historian, spent his youth in the château here. He switched sides from Burgundy to the service of Louis XI of France, and was given honours and estates, only to lose them and be sent to the appalling swinging cage prisons for eight months (*see* History, page 27). He bounced back as a favourite under Charles VIII. He was the father of French historians.

Comines has a historic fête on the second Sunday in October – Fête des Louches, when beribboned ladles (*louches*) are thrown from the top of the town hall to celebrate the rescue of a local lord who, when imprisoned, told his friends he was there by throwing his spoons out of the window after each meal.

COMPIÈGNE
[Oise]

A delightful town, splendidly situated on the banks of the Oise
river near where it meets the Aisne, beside a beautiful forest of
oak and beech which dates from Charlemagne. Understandably
it has been a favourite hide-out of kings since Charles the Bald
built a palace and founded an abbey there in the ninth century.

The royal palace which stands there now was ranked third
after Versailles and Fontainebleau. Louis XIV liked to relax
there. 'At Versailles I am a king,' he said, 'at Fontainebleau a
prince, but here I am a peasant.' He stayed there seventy-five
times and each time there was an ostentatious fête.

A more modest château stood there in the fourteenth century, built in 1374 by Charles V of France.

In May 1430 the Burgundians and the English camped on
the north bank of the Oise, under the walls of Compiègne. Joan
of Arc returned to Compiègne on 23 May, entered the town
from the south, and that evening at 5 p.m. made a sortie, crossing the river by a bridge standing at the end of what is now rue
Jeanne d'Arc. She drove the advance guard of the Burgundians
from their camp but they brought up reserves, and the English
slipped along the river to cut off her retreat. She had nearly got
back to the drawbridge over the Oise when she was wounded by
an archer and taken prisoner by the Burgundians. The place
where she was caught is now place du 54e Régiment d'In-
fanterie, where there is a statue of her on a horse.

Louis XV decided to enlarge the château into a palace by
almost total reconstruction. Jacques Gabriel, and later his son
Jacques Ange Gabriel, who designed the Petit Trianon and place
de la Concorde, were the architects, but they were handicapped
by the town ramparts and buildings and had to use a rather
awkward triangular plan. The design is a little severe but
imposing. Louis XV died before it was finished. Louis XVI
finished it in 1785 – four years before the Revolution. In 1770,
four years before he became king, he went to the palace to meet
for the first time the princess who was to be his bride – Marie-
Antoinette, youngest daughter of the Empress Marie Theresa,
and he was so paralysed by shyness that he would not look at

her. Marie-Antoinette designed the decoration of her own apartments, but was beheaded before she had slept in them.

Napoleon, of course, was not so timid. He took a fancy to Compiègne as an imperial residence and had it renovated. He married his second wife, Marie-Louise of Austria (niece of the unfortunate Marie-Antoinette), by proxy in 1810, then she came from Vienna to France to join him. She was to have supper and stay in Soissons on her way to Paris for the wedding ceremony, but he met her carriage near Compiègne in the pouring rain, smothered her with affection, and whipped her off to Compiègne Palace for supper and the night. Their official wedding ceremony at St Cloud a few days later was something of a formality.

In 1814, 18,000 Prussians attacked Compiègne. They were repulsed by 1200 French soldiers guarding the palace. The palace reached its heyday in the reign of Napoleon III and Princess Eugénie, who loved Compiègne and held extravagant balls, masques, hunting parties, soirées and every sort of entertainment there against a background of political and amorous intrigues. The Emperor chartered trains to take his guests to Compiègne. They included famous commoners such as Louis Pasteur and Alexandre Dumas as well as nobles. The beautiful life ended abruptly when Napoleon declared war on Prussia in 1870 and the Prussians invaded. He and his Empress were soon living beside the common in Chislehurst, Kent, in a house which is now a golf-club pavilion.

The royal and Napoleonic apartments are on the first floor of the palace, overlooking views of the park to the forest. They are full of Napoleon I period (First Empire) furniture, fine tapestries and many souvenirs of various reigns. The Grands Apartements have wood panellings with mythological themes painted by Girodet (1767–1827) who later gave up good painting to write boring poetry. Tapestries are superb, sculptures, silks, carved bronzes, porcelain and chandeliers are all very splendid. Marie-Antoinette's games room (*salon de jeu*) has been restored to its pre-Revolutionary original condition, with almost transparent curtains and Lyon silk hangings – all very pretty. The huge ballroom prepared for the marriage of Napoleon and Marie-Louise has a barrel-vaulted roof with paintings showing

Napoleon's victories. In the guest wing is a museum of Napoleon III (Second Empire). There is a painting of Empress Eugénie and her Maids of Honour in which the girls look incredibly life-like – by the German Franz Winterhalter (1805–73), a very successful court painter in Paris.

In the kitchen courtyard, now glass-roofed, is a most interesting Musée de la Voiture – a display of horse-drawn carriages and early motor-cars from Louis XV's reign onwards. There are stage coaches (*diligences*), the King of Spain's coach (1740), a post-chaise, superb sledges, a remarkable steam coach (1895) and priceless cars. These include steam cars from De Dion and Trepardoux, the 1914 torpedo-shaped Sigma-Ballot, forerunner of later racing cars, Panhard Numero 2 (the second built, with a Daimler engine), a Bollée driven in the 1985 Paris–Marseilles race, and the remarkable 'Jamais Contente', fitted with pneumatic Michelin tyres, which reached 100kmph in 1899. You can see the original small Renault of 4hp (1900) and the half-tracked Citroën which in 1924 was the first car to cross the Sahara and the African continent. There is a wonderful collection of bicycles, from a hobby horse of 1817 and the 'grand-bi' (penny-farthing bike with an enormous front wheel) – the first pedal cycle. (The palace is shut on Tuesday.)

West of the palace is the fine late-Gothic town hall, which has an unusual belfry from which wooden figures appear by clock-work to mark the hours and quarters. Inside is the Musée de la Figurine, a fascinating collection of toy soldiers, some of well-known military men. There are painted dioramas of famous battles (shut Monday). Musée Vivenel near the river (shut Tuesday) has fine Greek vases, medieval religious art, eighteenth- to nineteenth-century furniture and ceramics, and a collection of drawings and paintings from around Europe.

Nearby is the Beauregard Tower, most unfortunately named considering that Joan of Arc was imprisoned there after her capture in 1430.

Compiègne Forest is delightful. Its broad grassy avenues are lined with beautiful oaks and beeches. I have wandered happily in it for hours, both on foot and driving, coming upon secret ponds and little lakes, brooks, glades and peaceful hamlets.

On its northern edge, 7km from Compiègne, is Clairière

l'Armistice, a clearing in the woods with a monument, near the village of Rethondes. Here on 11 November 1918, Marshal Foch and the Germans signed the Armistice ending the First World War. They signed it in a railway carriage in a siding. In revenge, Hitler insisted that the French surrender in 1940 should be signed in the same carriage. The carriage was later taken to Berlin, where it was destroyed as the Allies approached. The carriage which stands there now is a replica, but with genuine objects inside. In 1940 the German staff wisely had the train in which Hitler himself was accommodated moved to the mouth of a tunnel in case the RAF chose to join in the party.

Compiègne Forest still covers 15,000 hectares, 20,000 with the forest of Laigue across the river Aisne. It is criss-crossed by avenues, some for driving, others of grass for walking or horse-riding. You can park your car and follow yellow-marked walking tracks for two hours, reach the rugged heart of the forest, and still find your car again.

From avenue Royale in Compiègne, take route Tournante to the left into avenue des Beaux Monts, then at Renard Carrefour (crossroads) turn right on route Eugénie, which later rejoins avenue Beaux Monts. A signposted road left will take you to Les Beaux Monts, famous for its trees and its view.

From Compiègne you can drive on minor roads through the Compiègne, Laigue and St Gobain Forests, most of the way to Laon (see page 155). There are guided nature walks in the forest (apply at the Tourist Office).

TOURIST INFORMATION place Hôtel-de-Ville
(44.40.01.00)
MARKETS Wednesday, Saturday
FESTIVALS 1 May – Fête Muguet (Cavalcade, floral floats, fête Joan of Arc); end May – les Séries de Compiègne (named after Napoleon III's series of fêtes); end September – son et lumière; 11 November – Armistice celebrations at La Clairière

HOTELS

Flandres, 16 quai République (44.83.24.40). Beside river. Renovated. Solid comfort. Established under Louis XIV. ROOMS C–D. MEALS B–E. (Restaurant under separate ownership.)

France et Restaurant Chat Qui Tourne, 17 rue Floquet
(44.40.02.74). Some rooms simple. Classical cooking, good
value. Logis. ROOMS B–D. MEALS B–G.
Hostellerie Royal Lieu, at Royallieu, 2km S on rue Senlis
(44.20.10.24). Lovely hotel. Comfortable rooms opening on to
garden with forest beyond. Quiet. Pricey. Very good meals.
ROOMS E–F. MEALS E–G.

RESTAURANT
Rethondes
8km E from Compiègne by the N31, in forest (see text).
Auberge du Pont (Alain Blot), near Armistice coach (44.85.60.24).
Cooking full of good ideas. Pricey. MEALS F–G. Shut Saturday
lunch, Sunday evening, Monday.

Choisy-au-Bac
5km NE from Compiègne by D66.
Étangs du Buissonnet (44.40.17.41). Attractive, by lake, nice out-
look. Very good classical cooking. Expensive. MEALS F–G. Shut
2–16 November; Sunday evening, Monday.

CONDÉ-EN-BRIE
[AISNE]

Because of its association with the Condé family of Bourbon
royal blood, this agricultural village 15km SE of Château-
Thierry, at the meeting of the valleys of the rivers Surmelin and
Dhuys, was renamed Vallon Libre after the Revolution. It has an
old market-hall on Doric columns and a château built in the
sixteenth century by Louis de Bourbon-Vendôme, Bishop of
Laon, who left it to his nephew Louis de Bourbon, the first
Prince de Condé. It was much remodelled in the eighteenth
century and still contains the old prince's apartments, as decorated and furnished then, with rare furniture. Louis XV furniture and decorations in the Grand Salon are also well worth
seeing. The music room was designed by a famous decorator,
Servandoni (open daily July, August; Sunday from Easter to 30
June, September to 31 October).

CONDÉ-SUR-L'ESCAUT
[Nord]

Old fortified town 13km N of Valenciennes on the D935, often besieged. Some of its ramparts, and an austere fifteenth-century château, remain. Just N is the pleasant Bonsecours-France Forest, with marked paths and a lagoon, much appreciated by the people of industrial Valenciennes. In it is a fine château – Château de l'Ermitage, with 200 windows. It was built by Louis XV for the Duc de Croy. The Belgian border is on the north end of the forest at Bon-Secours, which is in Belgium. Its basilica is a celebrated place of pilgrimage.

CORBIE
[Somme]

Corbie Abbey was once so important that the abbots held the title of Count and could make and issue money. On the Somme, 16km E of Amiens, the abbey was founded by St Bathilde, wife of the Frankish King Clovis in AD657, and played a very important part in the spread of Christianity in northern Europe. Most of it was knocked down in the Revolution. The superb façade of the abbey-church of St Pierre shows its importance as a work of Gothic art in the fifteenth century. Its 55-metre-high towers frame three doorways topped by a superb late-Gothic rose window. Unfortunately, it is reduced to the size of its old nave. Inside are fine statues from the fifteenth to sixteenth centuries.

St Collette, who reformed the order of St Claire in the fifteenth century and founded seventeen convents, including one in Amiens, was born in Corbie. Her home has gone, but a chapel was built in 1959 on the site.

With the Somme on its doorstep, the Ancre river northward and the Hallué to the west, this area is called 'three Valleys'.

Market Friday

COUCY-LE-CHÂTEAU
[AISNE]

I do wish that I had seen Château de Coucy before the First World War. I have seen pictures and it must have been a very proud and formidable pile indeed, with its huge cylindrical keep, four strong, round defence towers and high, thick walls enfolding the village. Certainly the man who built it in 1230–42, Enguerrand III, was a proud man. *'Roi ne suis, ne Prince, ne Duc, ne Comte aussi. Je suis le Sire de Coucy'* ('I am not king, nor prince, nor duke, nor count – I am the Sire of Coucy').

Alas, Coucy stands 17km N of Soissons and was in the front line in 1917. The Germans blew up the tower – 'the most beautiful cylindrical keep in Europe'.

You can see how enormous the castle was from the great gatehouse Porte de Laon, and the size of the remains. The tower was 31 metres round and 54 metres high. The walls reach 7 metres in thickness, and there is a well 65 metres deep which kept the inhabitants watered. Despite the great damage, the remains are still worth seeing.

In the museum is a good model of the town and castle; old drawings and photos, and little models of people in costume.

Domaine de la Gougère is the garden of the house where Gabrielle d'Estrées, Duchesse de Beaufort, the beautiful and intelligent favourite mistress of Henri IV, gave birth in 1594 to their son, César, who became Duc de Vendôme.

Coucy is now called Coucy-le-Château Auffrique. The D13 northward is an attractive road joining others which run through the Basse Forêt de Coucy, and to the NE the very beautiful St Gobain Forest.

Follow the D1 NW and turn right on to the D934 through Bois du Montoir. Here is the base where the Germans hid their massive gun 'Big Bertha'. On 23 March 1918, it shelled Paris – 123km away – for the first time.

CRÉCY-EN-PONTHIEU
[Somme]

Such a peaceful little town to evoke the name of such a bloody and historic battle. On 26 August 1346, at the beginning of the Hundred Years War, Edward III of England and his army, marching from Normandy, were met by a French force under King Philippe VI, including all the leading knights of northern France. The English had hundreds of archers; the French had few. Edward directed his forces from a windmill on a hilltop. When the battle became fierce, he sent in his sixteen-year-old son, the Black Prince, to command a wing of the English Army. The lad was remarkable. His black armour and crest seen on battlefields afterwards brought misgivings to all enemies. The French lost 20,000 men, including 1300 knights of noble blood. The brave but foolhardy blind King Jean of Bohemia insisted upon fighting, tied to his horse, to show his loyalty to King Philippe, who was his brother. He was, of course, killed. He was buried where he fell and the cross of Bohemia raised over his grave. Instead of the customary war memorial to the fallen of the two world wars, in Crécy's main street there is a memorial inscribed 'To the memory of the Frenchmen who died for their fatherland, 26 August 1346', with a tribute to Jean, King of Bohemia, on the back.

There is little else to mark the battle. The windmill has long gone. Above the fields of grain is a *table d'orientation* and the flags of France, Bohemia and Luxemburg, with the Union Jack – *not* the cross of St George of England: the French have obviously forgotten that Edward III was forced to spend even more time fighting the Scots than he spent fighting the French.

Crécy is in a delightful position for anyone wanting a restful day or two before pressing on southward or northward. The attractive D938 eastward from the N1 takes you there in 11km, and it is right on the edge of the lovely Crécy Forest, which has a web of little pathways and lanes and one very attractive road (D111) through it to Lamotte Bouleux. You can turn right off D111 at the Monument crossroads to Forest-Montiers, a hamlet on the N1 where St Riquier set up a hermitage which became a convent. François I's son died there of the plague, aged twenty-three.

The little river Maye runs through Crécy, only about 5km from its source. It continues past the north edge of the forest to the lakes near Bernay-en-Ponthieu (*see* page 98) and to the Somme estuary at Le Crotoy (*see* page 126)

MARKET Monday

HOTEL

Maye, 13 rue St Riquier (22.23.54.35). Simple modern Logis with good-value simple meals. ROOMS B–D. MEALS A–D. Shut February holidays; Sunday evening, Monday low season.

CREIL
[OISE]

Iron and industrial town on two banks of the Oise and an island which, like the left bank, is partly wooded. Creil is only 8km N of Chantilly on the N16.

Its Gallé-Juillet museum (allée Musée) is unusually interesting. It is in an eighteenth-century house with original décor, beautiful furniture and fine ceramics, Delft ware and porcelain (shut Tuesday).

2km N is another industrial town, Nogent-sur-Oise, which has a twelfth- to thirteenth-century church with a belltower built in 1130. It also has a hotel Sarcus with a nightclub open all night (La Vinci).

Monetair, 3km SW, is really part of Creil's industrial complex. It specializes in sheet metal for the car industry.

TOURIST INFORMATION place Gén. de Gaulle, Creil
(44.55.16.07)
MARKET Wednesday, Thursday, Saturday
FESTIVAL First Sunday in November – Chestnut Fair

HOTELS

Martinez, 9 ave Jules Uhry (44.55.00.39). Modern, near station. No restaurant. ROOMS C–D.

Nogent

Sarcus, 7 rue Châteaubriand (44.74.01.31). Modern, in park; nightclub. ROOMS D–E. MEALS C–F. Shut 25 July–21 August. Restaurant shut Saturday lunch, Sunday.

CRÉPY-EN-VALOIS
/[OISE]

Crépy is in a very rich agricultural area, on the western end of the Retz Forest, and only 8km from the Compiègne Forest by a delightful road, the D116, which is far more pleasant than the busier D352.

The D116 joins a whole network of delightful little roads through the forest, some leading to the fine old château at Pierrefonds (*see* page 179), others to Compiègne itself (*see* page 115).

Valois was one of the ancient 'Pays de France' and its lords became Kings of France. The first was Philippe VI (1328–50), who lost the battle of Crécy. The last, Henri III, was assassinated in 1589 and followed by Henri IV, first of the Bourbons. It was the Valois King Charles VIII who, though failing in an Italian military campaign, brought back an admiration for Italian decoration and design, imported Italians to decorate his château at Amboise and sowed the first seeds of the Renaissance in France.

All that remains of the château of the Dukes of Valois is two towers, rooms housing the museum and St Aubin's chapel. The Valois King Henri II preferred Villers-Cotterets to Crépy, which then began to lose importance.

The church of St Thomas has its tall fifteenth-century spire and its façade. It was the first church dedicated to St Thomas à Becket, the Archbishop of Canterbury murdered in his cathedral. When Thomas had fled from England earlier, he stayed at Crépy with the Comte de Valois in his château. The Comte was having this church built and when Thomas was killed, he made a pilgrimage to his tomb and dedicated the church to him on his return.

The greatly altered twelfth-century Romanesque church of St Denis stands in front of the remains of the fifteenth-century abbey of St Arnould.

The museum in the château remains (open 15 March to 15 November except Tuesday), is called Musée du Valois et de l'Archerie, with a wonderful collection of bows and arrows through the centuries, from France, most other European countries, and Africa and the East, with flags of many Companies of Archers and archery trophies. Valois' Compagnies d'Archers are known throughout France, appearing at competitions and fêtes all over the country. Bouquet Provincial (Oise archery contest) is held in a different village each year.

The museum also has religious images rescued from defunct or destroyed churches.

TOURIST INFORMATION 7 rue Soissons (44.59.03.97).

MARKET Wednesday morning

HOTELS

Relais de Valois, 4 place du Paon (44.59.11.21). When it was the locally renowned 'Trois Pigeons', I used to drink there with the locals. The bedrooms were improved in 1986, and it reverted to its old name from the days when stage-coaches changed horses here. However, it still serves *pigeonneau à la Valoise*. ROOMS C. MEALS A–E. Shut February; Sunday evening, Monday out of season.

Hostellerie de Geresme, 1 ave Europe (44.39.63.04). Was once a priory; attractive, old comfortable rooms. Quiet. ROOMS C–D. MEALS C–F.

LE CROTOY
[SOMME]

A delightful little place on the Somme estuary where you can stroll along the quai Léonard to watch the fishing boats land their catch, then wander across for a fish meal. Prawns, langoustines, mussels, cockles, crabs are all superb, but a lot of white fish is landed, too, especially plaice, dabs, herring. Eels, too.

Though it is not a pretty place, the road to Le Cortoy round the bay from St-Valery-sur-Somme has super views over les Mollières, the salt marshes which produce the succulent pré-salé lamb. The D940 N to Rue is less interesting.

Another way of travelling between Le Crotoy and St Valery is by the Chemin de Fer de la Baie de la Somme – a grand name for a little railway which has both steam- and diesel-engines but runs only from early July to mid-September, on Saturday and Sunday. The 14km route from St Valery crosses the Somme canal and gives good views of the Somme bay, stopping at Noyelles-sur-Mer, then Le Crotoy.

When Joan of Arc was moved from prison in the old château in Le Crotoy to St Valery on her way to Rouen in 1430, she was taken across by boat. There was no road then. The castle has long since gone.

Le Crotoy has a beach with sands stretching for 10km, and is a family holiday resort, but the harbour is the great lure. Thirty or so *chalutiers* (tiny trawlers) are based here and come and go twice a day. They are joined these days by pleasure boats and the scene is lively. Lots of fishermen line the quai and banks, fishing for plaice and eels. The river Maye is canalized 2km N of Le Crotoy until it reaches the bay. The quay, pier and place Jeanne d'Arc form a pedestrian area.

Alas, the great Mado has retired from the quayside Baie hotel restaurant Chez Mado. I feel sorry for anyone who never met her in her glory, sailing round like a great schooner dressed in pearls, or who never tasted her superlative fish. I know nothing of her successor except that prices are, according to my French sources, *'redoutables'* – formidable.

The winds in the bay make Le Crotoy a good centre for sailing, windsurfing, and wind sailing on the sands.

TOURIST INFORMATION digue J. Noiret (high season – 22.27.81.97)

MARKETS Tuesday, Friday

DESVRES
[PAS-DE-CALAIS]

The little industrial town where the famous Desvres china (*faience*) has been made since the eighteenth century is not pretty, but is in the centre of a lovely forest and countryside. Its products are mostly copies of old designs of Delft, Nevers, Rouen, Moustiers and Strasbourg. You can see good examples in four rooms in the town hall.

Desvres has a huge market square which slopes down the valley. Many seasonal markets are held for farm animals, and there are also regular markets for farm produce, especially dairy products and vegetables.

Desvres Forest to the north is planted with a mixture of trees. There are marked paths for walkers covering 12km, two forest roads for driving and the very pleasant D127 which remains attractive most of the way to Guines in the north. In the NW corner of the forest is the charming little village of Crémarest, which has several old houses, including Manoir de Fresnoye, with one square tower and one hexagonal, and a twelfth-century church with a six-stage tower, 29 metres high, added in the sixteenth century. Alongside is the trout-river Liane. Small roads W lead to the bigger Boulogne Forest.

S from Desvres the pretty D127 continues through the valley of another trout river, the Course, almost to Montreuil.

DOUAI
[NORD]

Douai is much maligned. I confess to avoiding it for years. In the heart of the old coal-mining area, which looks no better now even though it produces little coal, almost totally wrecked in two world wars, hemmed in by big main roads rumbling with lorries, with the old N43 actually running through it to Cambrai, and with a mind-bending one-way traffic system, Douai seemed to me to have everything stacked against it.

The A1 and A26 motorways have relieved it of a lot of traffic, but it still has to carry the important industrial traffic going south-east to Metz and Saarbrücken in Germany.

I fell in love right away with Douai's fifteenth century town-hall belfry – a delightful piece of ostentatious Gothic, flaunting itself like an overdressed actress. 'So amusing, so mad, so alive', said Victor Hugo in 1837, and it still is. The jangle of its bells on each quarter and hour seems to be a song of defiance to the enemies that have tried to destroy this old Flemish town – wars and industry.

Through a succession of booms and depressions, bombardments and occupations, this old Flemish town has kept up its spirits, so obvious in its annual carnival Le Cortège des Gayants. On the second Sunday in July, five giants in costume of the Middle Ages are carried through the town by folkloric groups. There are Gayant the father, 7½ metres tall, made in 1538 and the pride of the town, Marie Caregon, his wife, 6½ metres tall, and their children Jacquot, Binbin and Filion. This heralds a week of feasting, parties, concerts, ballets, folk dancing, organ recitals and carillon concerts from the belfry, finishing with a revue and firework display.

The belfry has sixty-two bells on its fourth floor, replacing famous bells destroyed by the Germans in 1917. On the hour they play what the locals call 'a Scottish Puritan Air'. On the half-hour they play a barcarolle. On the quarter- and three-quarter-hours they play 'L'Air de Gayant'. The bells give concerts each Saturday morning, and recitals on Monday evening in June, July, August, and on fête or fair days.

You can climb the belfry (192 steps) to view the industrial

wastelands around Douai (on Sunday all the year, daily 1 April to 31 August). You see also the town hall with its eighteenth-century Gothic council chamber, and its cellars.

The wonderful and famous painting of Douai's belfry by Corot is in the Louvre in Paris. By careful reconstruction Douai has kept its eighteenth-century flavour, with superb eighteenth-century buildings. This has, of course, meant narrow streets with traffic problems. The imposing Collegiate church of St Pierre has a huge stone belfry tower built in the sixteenth to seventeenth centuries. The Ancienne Chartreuse is a fine group of sixteenth- to eighteenth-century buildings surrounding a small cloister with an especially interesting mansion, Abancourt-Montmorency, in Flemish Renaissance style.

The museum is in this old charterhouse in a lovely setting. Despite great losses when the old museum was destroyed in the Second World War, the exhibits here are excellent. The ceramics are particularly interesting, coming from a wide range of sources from Sèvres, Nevers and St Omer to India, China and Japan. Dutch and Flemish paintings are very good, too. Look at the lovely landscape background to Salomon le Bray's panel painting *Rebecca and Eliezer*. In later paintings, the landscapes of Isabey, Jongkind and Boudin are delightful. Both the river Scarpe and the Sensée canal cross the town, and walks by the quays of the river past old buildings are pleasant.

TOURIST INFORMATION 70 place d'Armes
(27.88.26.79)
MARKETS Daily
FESTIVALS First two weeks July – Cortège des Gayants
(see text); Second Sunday in July – procession; 15
August – second-hand fair (Brocante)

HOTELS

Terrasse, 36 terrasses St Pierre (27.88.70.04). 'Three-chimney' Logis de France in a quiet square by the church of St Pierre. One of the best eating places in Douai. Prices have risen. ROOMS E–F. MEALS E–G.

RESTAURANTS

Turbotin, 9 rue Massue (27.87.04.16). Loved by locals, rather

formal, excellent fish. Wide range of menus except Saturday.
MEALS B–F. Shut August; Sunday evening, Monday.
Buffet Gare (27.88.99.26). Station buffet restaurant. Good value.
MEALS A–D. Shut Saturday in summer; Sunday and Monday
evenings.

DOULLENS
[SOMME]

A very pleasant little town on the river Authie, 32km N of
Amiens, with gabled houses in brick and stone which give it a
look of Picardie.

In the town hall here on 26 March 1918, a conference took
place which changed history. The great German offensive
under Ludendorff had been so successful that there was talk in
France of suing for peace, and both politicians and generals in
France and Britain were arguing about the future conduct of
the war. Foch was Supreme Commander of the French, Douglas
Haig that of the British, and they had different military ideas.
Suddenly, in a room packed with politicians and top-brass
generals, the normally stubborn Scot, Haig, said in a deliberate
voice, 'If General Foch consents to give me his advice, I shall be
pleased to take it.' Foch became Allied Commander-in-Chief,
bickering stopped and the next offensive won the war. It was a
lesson well learned in the Second World War for the invasion of
France. A stained-glass window and two paintings by Jornas in
the United Command Room recall the scene.

François I built the citadel in Doullens in 1525 as defence
against the Spanish, who were occupying Artois. Strengthened
by later kings, it suddenly lost its importance when Artois was
ceded to France in 1659, and became a State prison. Now it is
open to the public daily 1 May to 30 September and is interesting for the original section, underground tunnels and the view
from the ramparts.

MARKET Thursday

HOTEL

Bons Enfants, 23 rue d'Arras (22.77.06.58). Simple family-run, cheap Logis. MEALS A–C. MEALS A–D. Restaurant shut Saturday

DUNKERQUE
[*See* Major Towns, page 54]

EPPE-SAUVAGE
[NORD]

A delightful, peaceful place in the Avesnois among pastures and woods, very near to the Belgian frontier. Few tourists find it and traffic is very light, so it is a good place for a rest. The rivers Helpe-Majeur and Eau d'Eppe meet there. To the south-west the Helpe river gets broader, and marshes and lakes appear, including the large Lac du Joly, made by damming the river. It stretches almost to Liessies. Val Joly has a good centre for watersports and pleasure craft, and its banks are mostly beautifully wooded.

RESTAURANT

Goyère, rue Verdun (27.61.80.11). In eighteenth-century house. Very popular locally. Good value. MEALS A–F. Shut Tuesday evening, Wednesday.

ERMENONVILLE
[OISE]

At the SE edge of Ermenonville Forest, which runs S from Senlis, the little village of Ermenonville on the N330 is celebrated all over France for its park, attached to the charming Louis XV château where the Dukes of Girardin lived from 1763 until the 1930s.

In May 1778, Jean-Jacques Rousseau, whose writings did

much to inspire the French Revolution, visited the Marquis, took great delight in the natural gardens, and stayed in a pavilion in the grounds, spending his time giving music lessons to the Marquis' children and walking in the park and the forest beyond it. He died suddenly in July. He was sixty-six. The Marquis, a great admirer, buried him in the Isle of Poplars, a tiny island on the garden lake. Although the body was exhumed and taken to the Panthéon in Paris in 1794, the tomb is still there and is a shrine of pilgrimage. Napoleon asked the Marquis to take him to see it. 'It would have been better for the peace of France if that man had never existed,' said Napoleon. 'He prepared the Revolution.'

'It is not for you to condemn the Revolution,' said the Marquis.

'The future will say that it would have been better for the world if neither he nor I had existed,' said Napoleon.

The garden is simple, on the English pattern rather than a formalized French garden. It is made up mostly of trees with paths, the lake and a number of 'monuments' fashionable in the eighteenth century, such as a Temple of Philosophy. In 1938 the Touring Club de France bought the estate to prevent it being split up for building sites. It is open daily except Tuesday and has a campsite at the south end.

3km N are the romantic ruins of thirteenth-century Abbey of Chaalis, surrounded by forest and lakes. In the eighteenth century a spendthrift abbot had built for himself by Aubert, architect of the beautiful Chantilly stables, a small château, which now houses a mixed museum, with Egyptian and Gallo-Roman antiquities, paintings, sculptures and Renaissance furniture. Rooms are also devoted to Rousseau.

Between the park and the abbey is Mer de Sable, a sand desert where an actor, Jean Richard, set up an amusement park and a good, small zoo (open end March to 15 September except Friday). Nearby is the Désert – sand, trees, lakes, briar – where the Marquis had some of Rousseau's writings inscribed in stone.

Ermenonville Forest joins Chantilly Forest.

HOTELS

Prieuré (44.54.00.44). Lovely eighteenth-century house once belonging to the church, hides behind a high stone wall. No restaurant. ROOMS G.

Croix d'Or, 2 rue Prince Radziwill (44.54.00.04). Simple Logis. Mentioned by the writer Alexandre Dumas (*Three Musketeers, Count of Monte Cristo*) in his memoirs. Get a back room to avoid traffic noise. ROOMS B–C. MEALS C–E. Shut 2–13 January; Monday.

ESQUELBECQ
[NORD]

Quiet little town on the river Yser, just off the D916 S of Dunkerque, Esquelbecq is typically Flemish, with a huge church, paved main square and low houses with brown-tiled roofs, mostly decorated with flowers.

The river feeds the moat of the thirteenth-century brick feudal château, which has nine pepper-pot towers, stepped gables and a huge 45-metre-high guard tower (open afternoons 15 April to 15 October).

The twelfth-century Romanesque church has a striking brick façade and triple nave.

RESTAURANT

Relais du Château, 11 Grand'Place (28.65.62.87). In fine old house in main square. MEALS C–E.

ESTRÉE
[PAS-DE-CALAIS]

Just off the D127 on a Roman road, near Montreuil, with the little Course river dividing it over a small bridge from Estréelles. The two towns are also divided by history. In the Wars of Religion, Estréelles was Protestant, Estrée Catholic, and they still hardly talk to each other. They have separate churches, separate schools, separate mayors, separate fête days. Even their joint war memorial on the bridge has the names of the dead of each village on separate lists pointing opposite ways. And they have separate cemeteries. You can tell that Estrée is Catholic by the highly ornamented tombs.

HOTEL

Relais de la Course (21.06.18.04). Simple, real village inn with simple bedrooms, good-value, straightforward meals. Huge open fire in dining-room. ROOMS B. MEALS B–C. Shut Sunday evening.

ÉTAPLES
[PAS-DE-CALAIS]

'Eatapples', the Tommies of the First World War called it. They were taken there when badly wounded and at least 11,000 of them never left. They are buried in the cemetery, men of many nations, friend and foe. It was also a notorious training centre, the largest in France for British troops, with 100,000 men going through a fortnight's training under NCOs so bullying that there were mass demonstrations in September 1917, bordering on mutiny, which the War Office always denied happened. When the BBC did a programme on it in 1986, most newspapers printed outraged articles implying that the BBC was pumping out left-wing propaganda. But it *did* happen – those who had fathers or uncles in the Army in that war knew that it did. Because of the training depot the Germans bombed Étaples.

Today, however, Étaples is a busy and lively little fishing port and commercial centre, with ship-repair yards. It is in the estuary of the river Canche, joined by a bridge to Le Touquet, the seaside resort, and all the traffic leaving Le Touquet to go north to Boulogne or eastward to Montreuil and Hesdin has to cross the river there on this one bridge, so traffic is formidable in summer. Everything is done to persuade motorists to stick to the N39 going east along the river to avoid bringing the already busy market square to a standstill. Étaples is not an attractive place, but it is interesting. On the quay where the fishing boats land their catch is a good little fish market with an excellent fish restaurant run by the fishermen's association.

MARKETS Tuesday, Friday
FESTIVALS Every other year in August – Festival du
Hareng d'Or (golden herring) with blessing of the sea;
October – Joutes à Canots (rowing dinghy jousting) on
the Canche

HOTELS

Lion d'Argent, place de Gaulle (21.94.60.99). Very old inn. Good-value meals. ROOMS C. MEALS B–D. Shut Monday evening, Tuesday.

RESTAURANT

Pêcheurs d'Étaples, quai de la Canche (21.94.06.90). See text. Picture windows give views of river and boats. MEALS B–E.

FELLERIES
[SOMME]

Little town NE of Avesnes-sur-Helpe by the N133 and D80. Since the seventeenth century it has specialized in wood-turning and carving (Bois-Jolis). All sorts of items are made, from bobbins for textile mills to cruets. In an old water-mill is an exhibition of Bois-Jolis, attractive wooden items (open Sunday afternoon 1 April to 30 November; every day in July, August).

FÈRE-EN-TARDENOIS
[AISNE]

Small town important in Gallo-Roman days, on the river Ourcq, NE of Château-Thierry by the D967. It has superb sixteenth-century market-buildings in the town centre with large tiled roofs and fine timber work supported by stone pillars. The roofs had to be mended after damage in the First World War when the British General French made his headquarters in the town in 1914. The Germans took it briefly in 1918.

The sixteenth-century church, much restored, has very good carved wooden furniture from the seventeenth century. But the great sight of the town is the Château de Fère.

Of the thirteenth-century fortress, seven ruined towers remain – now part of the garden of the attractive great country-house-style château built by Anne de Montmorency, the exceedingly rich and powerful Constable of France, in the sixteenth century. He was given the estate by King François I. Montmorency collected châteaux. He had 130. He turned the old moat into a monumental pond. After one of his descendants was executed, having fallen out with Richelieu, Louis XIII gave it to the Prince of Condé. It passed by heritage and marriage to Louis-Philippe, Duc d'Orleans, gambler, lover of women, friend of Britain's Prince Regent. He popularized the old English sports of horse-racing and hard drinking in France, gave away a lot to the poor, and went to prison for debt. He joined the French Revolution, calling himself Philippe Égalité (Equality), became Deputy for Paris, voted for the execution of the King and knocked down a wing of his Fère Château to show how 'equal' he was. He was still guillotined because his son deserted to the Austrians. Ironically, his son, after living in Twickenham, became King Louis-Philippe, France's 'citizen-king', friend of Queen Victoria. The citizens got tired of him and he fled to England as 'Mr Smith'.

The château was very well restored last century, although the new wing is nothing like so splendid as the one knocked down by 'Mr Equality' and it looks a bit lop-sided. It has been a hotel for some years – a very expensive one, with fine antique furniture. You reach it by a climbing drive from the N367, 3km outside the town, in very quiet countryside, yet only a few miles N of the A4 Paris-Reims motorway. Unfortunately, the Blot family, who ran the hotel magnificently, sold it recently and a company now owns it. I have not tried it since.

HOTELS

Hostellerie du Château (23.82.21.13). See text. ROOMS G plus. MEALS G.

Auberge du Connétable (23.82.24.25). Opposite château's private drive. Down to earth. Old post-relais. Only three rooms. MEALS C–D. MEALS B–F. Shut February; Sunday evening, Monday.

LA FERTÉ-MILON
[AISNE]

A little town on a hill overlooking the river Ourcq on the edge of the Retz Forest. Jean Racine, the poet-playwright, was born there in 1639 to a family of minor aristocrats. His mother died when he was two. His father, a lawyer, went away and left him to be brought up in a very strict religious atmosphere by his grandmother, Marie Desmoulins, whose house is at 14 rue Reims in La Ferté-Milon. When she was widowed, she went to the famous Abbey of Port Royal and sent him to school at Beauvais. His sister's house is in the street now called after him, rue Jean-Racine. His statue in place Racine is by Jean d'Angers.

The town is overlooked by the rather stark ruins of its fortress, rebuilt in the fourteenth century by Louis d'Orleans, who had just finished rebuilding his château at Pierrefonds (*see* page 179) when his brother, King Charles VI, became deranged. Louis ruled France until he was murdered in 1407 by the soldiers of the Duke of Burgundy. In 1588 the extreme Catholic army of the Catholic League held out in the castle for six years against Henri IV, who finally took it and had its ramparts dismantled.

FILLIÈVRES
[PAS-DE-CALAIS]

A series of attractive '*villages fleuris*' line the D340 along the river Canche SE from Hesdin in Frévent. Fillièvres is one of the nicest. Just off the D340 by the D101, it is a village of red and ochre roofs among squelchy meadows, with a bulbous domed church, a delightful mill pond and a very modernized mill turned into a village inn, Auberge du Vieux Moulin, where you can take a glass of wine, beer or pernod at the bar with villagers, while old men pop in for tobacco and children for sweets and chocolate. The meals are of true old-style family cooking.

Further along the D340, at Couchy-sur-Canche, turn left on the D102 to reach Château de Flers, Louis XIV period with the chapel of the Barons de Flers (fifteenth century). The château now contains a riding school.

HOTEL

Vieux Moulin (21.47.93.42). See text. Friendly, simple, clean bedrooms. Very good value meals. ROOMS B–C. MEALS B–C.

FORT-MAHON-PLAGE
[SOMME]

Family seaside resort between Le Crotoy and Berck on the great sand stretch with dunes up to 30 metres high. It has a promenade and a long street lined with houses, small shops and cafés, many of them seasonal, selling the props of classic family holidays, such as spades, buckets, inflatable rings and dinghies, beach balls, and fast food, ice-creams, funny postcards and souvenirs. A little train runs around it – 'Fort-Mahon City Express'. Sand yachts use the beach.

At Quend Plage, 2km S, 'Aqualand' has been built. A system of glasshouses takes you from a huge indoor playground with adventure- and fun-pools (with waves, bubbling baths, geysers, slides, and kept at sub-tropical temperatures [28°C/82°F]) to an outdoor playground with three pools. It has refreshments, solarium and sauna. (Open early May to end September.)

Among the Grandes Dunes, the marshes north in the Baie d'Authie, and the canals and waterways of the Marquenterre bird park are some wonderful opportunities for bird watching. Wear boots or wellies.

HOTEL

Victoria (22.27.71.05). Fort-Mahon's original hotel. ROOMS B–E. MEALS A–F. Restaurant shut Sunday evening, Thursday.

RESTAURANT

Fiacre (22.27.76.30). Routhiauville, 2km inland on the D32. Formal restaurant in old farm. Sophisticated dishes. MEALS C–F. Shut 20–30 September; Tuesday evening, Wednesday except July, August.

FOURMIES
[NORD]

Little industrial town near the Belgian border N of Hirson, among forests and a number of small lakes good for fishing and boating (Étangs des Moines). An important textile town last century, it still has an exhibition of textile machines in working order and interesting photographs of the lives of families and workers over one hundred years. They are in a former cotton mill (L'Ecomusée – open 1 May to 31 October).

TOURIST INFORMATION place Verte (shut mornings
out of season – 27.60.40.97)
MARKET Saturday morning

HOTEL

Providence, 12 rue Verpraet (27.60.06.25). ROOMS C. MEALS A–D. Shut August; Saturday and Sunday evenings.

RESTAURANT

Auberge Étangs des Moines, 2km E by the D964 and local road (27.60.02.62). On lakeside. MEALS C–E. Shut two weeks in early September; mid-December–8 January; Sunday evening, Friday.

FRÉVENT
[PAS-DE-CALAIS]

After following the roads through '*villages fleuris*' from Hesdin along the Canche, Frévent is a bit grey and disappointing. But, an important wool town last century, it is an interesting place. It has a plastics factory now.

From 1137 to the Revolution, Frévent had a very important abbey. All that remains of it is a large avenue and a château. In 1588 negotiations took place in the abbey between the French, Spanish and English for the Treaty of Le Cateau-Cambrésis, which gave parts of Spanish Flanders and Artois to the French.

Knocked about in the Revolution, it was bought in 1823 by Baron de Fourment, who set up one of the biggest wool-spinning mills in France in it. Frévent prospered until a fire in the mill led to its transfer to the Arras road.

The château was built in 1740 by the architect Raoul Coigniard, who was responsible for several well-known buildings, including the Abbey of Valloires (*see* Argoules, page 82). In 1915 Général Foch set up his headquarters in the château during the Battle of Artois. It is a towerless, sober but impressive building. The public gardens are pleasant. They include the château moat, which is used for fun and games in the local carnival.

HOTEL

Amiens, route Doullens   (21.03.65.43). Logis. Bedrooms greatly improved. ROOMS B–D. MEALS A–E. Shut Saturday in winter.

FROISSY
[SOMME]

Hamlet on a bridge over the Somme canal 3km of S of Bray-sur-Somme, E of Amiens, which has a little train which runs to the stadium at Dompierre (1hr 30 minutes) on Sunday from Easter to end September and also Wednesday and Saturday from 15 July to end August. The trip includes a visit to a museum of military and industrial railways.

GRAVELINES
[NORD]

Popular with the people of Flanders as a seaside resort. The river Aa reaches the sea there, and the sea once surrounded the dunes on which the original fishing hamlet of Les Huttes was built. The port made by canalizing the Aa was fortified in 1160, and for centuries it was the port of St Omer. The river is canalized through to St Omer with branches off it to Dunkerque, 13km E of Gravelines, and Calais, 26km W.

The little fortified port 2km E was built by the Spaniards when they owned this area and called Petit Fort Philippe after their King Philippe II. It was called 'the town of smugglers' in Napoleonic days when English boats landed contraband on the dunes. After huge damage in the Second World War, when French units held off German Panzer Divisions for four days to help the Dunkerque evacuation, Petit Fort Philippe was rebuilt in Flemish style and is now a family bathing resort and a good marina. Petit Fort Philippe almost meets the great new Dunkerque harbour and industrial zone, still in its early stages. They

Water-mill at Gravelines

are divided by a nuclear power station. Grand Fort Philippe is at the other side of Gravelines, over the river.

When Gravelines became French in 1658 after the Battle of the Dunes, it was fortified by Vauban, Louis XIV's military architect, and a surprising amount of his ramparts have survived, very well preserved. The town did not have the money to knock them down. In Louis XIV's reign it was such an austere naval and military base that officers had a jingle: 'From the plague, from famine, from the garrisons of Bergues and of Gravelines, good Lord preserve us.'

For centuries Gravelines boats went fishing to the Newfoundland Banks and Iceland. Then the main fishing fleet deserted to Boulogne. Now there is a small fleet of little trawlers. In fact, Gravelines has become more and more a pleasure resort. It has a very modern Social-Cultural Centre with activities ranging from a baby clinic and nursery to a school of sailing, and it has built the largest sport and leisure centre in the north of France, called Sportica. This has a huge range of activities, including excellent indoor tennis courts, skating and ice-hockey on an indoor artificial rink made of silicon, swimming-pools, a 90-metre water slide and a basketball stadium.

TOURIST INFORMATION Town hall, place Charles Valentin (28.23.08.13)

HOTEL

Beau Rivage, 7 boul. Léo-Lagrange (28.23.12.21). Beside sea. ROOMS C–D. MEALS C–F.

RESTAURANT

Auberge La Sciérie, route de Gravelines, St Folquin, 4km S (28.65.29.44). Good fresh fish. MEALS B–G.

GUINES
[PAS-DE-CALAIS]

Take away the modern cars parked in the centre, and the main square of Guines could be a film-set for a First World War

French town. It is even called place Foch after the French commander-in-chief. But Guines' history is far older.

Guines is only 10km from Calais. Instead of catching the N43 to the A26 motorway or to St Omer, slip down the D127 on the right marked to Guines and running alongside a canal. Then, when you have had a look around Guines, take the D231 to Ardres. You will avoid a great deal of traffic and see something of this strange *marais* (marshy) countryside. Better still, continue on the D127 which runs very prettily past the Guines Forest and among hills and hamlets of the Parc Régional all the way to Desvres and Montreuil. See St Omer some other time.

When the English owned Calais for over 200 years, Guines was their frontier town – their front line against the French, who were down the road in Ardres, and their base for raiding parties to find food in the villages and loot Boulogne. They strengthened the castle built by the Count of Flanders and tried to make the whole town an impregnable fortress. When the Hapsburg Emperor Charles V, who ruled most of what is now Germany, Spain and its colonies, Burgundy, Flanders and the Netherlands, was so strong that he was threatening France in the early sixteenth century, François I of France and Henry VIII of England considered an alliance against him. In 1520 they met between Guines and Ardres in fields 3km SE of Guines, just off what is now the little D215.

Henry and François had only two things in common – a love of women and of ostentatious show. Their meeting was like a great party at which each tried to outshine the other in everything. It was called 'The Field of the Cloth of Gold' (*Le Camp du Drap d'Or*) because François hung his tents with gold-thread cloth, draped his horses with gold cloth and shod some with gold shoes. His courtiers were dressed in the most extravagant costumes. 6000 workmen prepared the site. The painter Jean Bourdichon designed the whole display.

Henry had built a palace in crystal, 'scintillating in the sun'. His 5000 followers were dressed in velvet, satin and gold. Cardinal Wolsey organized his display. Among items sent from England were 2014 sheep, 700 conger eels, 26 dozen heron and 4 bushels of mustard. Balls, feasts and tournaments went on from 7 June until 24 June. The two kings jousted every day. They had both brought their own choirs and they held a combined open-air mass. On 24 June the wind got up. It was too strong for jousting, so Henry and François wrestled. François threw Henry flat on his back. Then the wind blew down Henry's Crystal Palace. They parted swearing eternal peace. But Henry went off and renewed his alliance with Charles V, which lasted for five years until the defeat of François in Italy and the bankruptcy of France, when the English realized that Spain had grown too powerful.

In 1558, before taking Calais from the English, the Duc de Guise took Guines. Those French who had lived there under the English were thrown out, the strong castle was pulled down and new people settled there, half of them Protestants who had been thrown out of other towns – ironic, considering that the Duc de Guise was an extremist Catholic and his son the main instigator of the mass-murder of Protestants in the St Bartholomew's Night Massacre.

Adding to the atmosphere in Guines' main square is a typical 1860s' town hall and a real old French inn, Lion D'Or – which when I first put it into my book *Travellers' France* in the 1970s seemed totally unchanged since the Tommies drank there in the First World War. I felt as if I were the only Englishman to have eaten there since. Now it is popular with Britons for a last night in France at bargain prices.

A manor-house château, built in 1806 in Louis XV style, is now the centre for the four-star campsite at Bien Assise on the outskirts of Guines. This has a good-value restaurant open to the public.

In the Guines Forest southward along D127 is a column on a hillside to the men who made the first balloon crossing of the Channel in 1780, 129 years before Blériot's first plane crossing and those of the French Colonel Blanchard and the American Dr Jeffries. It is signposted 'La Colonne Blanchard'. The forest has fine walks among superb oaks, beeches, silver birches and hornbeams, growing closely in places.

HOTEL

Lion d'Or, 7 place Mar. Foch (21.35.20.51). See text. Bedrooms simple but comfortable. Meals very good value. ROOMS B–C. MEALS A–D. Shut Sunday lunch.

GUISE
[AISNE]

This cheerful little town agreeably sited on the Oise where the D946 crosses the N29, 27km NE of St Quentin, gave its name to a spine-chilling family, the Ducs de Guise. It was also the birthplace of the French Revolutionary leader Camille Desmoulins, fellow law student with Robespierre in Paris, who was finally guillotined on Robespierre's orders during the Terror.

Guise is now mostly a modern town, due to extensive damage in two world wars, but old parts still exist.

The castle, originally built in the eleventh century, was rebuilt by François de Guise in the sixteenth century, and strengthened by Vauban about a hundred years later. In the First World War it was used as a target for the German artillery when the French General Lanrezac was holding up the German advance in 1914, to enable the French to regroup for the Battle of the Marne.

In 1952 a group called Club de Vieux Manoir, dedicated to restoring historic buildings, took on the formidable task of rebuilding it, and it still is not finished, but you can visit it and look around.

The first Duc de Guise was made a duke by François I for crushing a revolt of starving peasants in Lorraine. The second, François (1519–68), a brilliant soldier who held Metz against Charles V and took Calais from the English, was leader of the Catholics with his brother Charles, Archbishop of Reims, and they repressed Protestantism savagely. Some of the Duke's men murdered Protestants while they were at prayer, which sparked off the Wars of Religion. After victories over the Protestant forces, he was assassinated by a Protestant when he was besieging Orleans. His son Henri was head of the extremist

Catholic League. He became all powerful when François II, the King, was still a boy. Guise was responsible for the appalling bloodbath at Amboise. After an amateurish Protestant revolt he had dozens of Protestants tortured, broken on the wheel and strung out from Amboise castle balconies. He would lead out the royal family and Court after dinner to watch their agony. Even his own wife warned: 'What vengeance is being stored for the future!' The stench of corpses finally drove the court from the castle.

Then, when the new young King Charles IX had asked them to Paris for a wedding, he organized the massacre of most of the Protestant leaders – the St Bartholomew's Night Massacre. That turned the Wars of Religion into a bloodbath.

When Henri III came to the throne, de Guise's Catholic League became more of a terror organization than a religious one. Their arch-enemy was Henri of Navarre, who later became King Henri IV. But Guise had a greater ambition – to become King himself. He became a spy for France's enemy, Philippe II of Spain, and plotted to take over in France. It was the defeat of the Armada by the English that foiled his plan. When the Armada sailed to Dunkerque to pick up a Spanish army to invade England, he took armed men into Paris against Henri III's orders to make sure that the French did not grab the opportunity to drive the Spaniards from Flanders.

When the Armada failed, de Guise lost his ally and his power. Henri III had him and his powerful brother, the Archbishop of Lorraine, murdered at Blois in the same year, 1588. One more duke, also called Henri (1614–64), hit the political scene by joining a revolt against Richelieu. He then tried to take Naples from the Spaniards, and was captured by them. When released, he returned to live quietly in Paris. The town of Guise must have been glad to be rid of them.

MARKET Saturday

HOTEL

Champagne-Picardie, 41 rue Godin (23.60.43.44). Elegant conversion of nineteenth-century house. Pretty garden. No restaurant. ROOMS D.

HAM
[Somme]

On the canalized Somme 20km SW of St Quentin, Ham – perversely – is known for sugar, which it extracts from the sugar beet grown in northern France.

A notorious château-prison, destroyed by the Germans in 1917, was built in the fifteenth century, with walls 11 metres thick behind which political prisoners were held, including, in the eighteenth century, the politician and writer the Comte de Mirabeau, whose own father had previously shut him up for debt, the deposed ministers of Charles X's government after the 1830 Revolution, and Louis-Napoleon Bonaparte, later the Emperor Napoleon III. After his abortive landing in Boulogne from England in 1840, Louis-Napoleon was moved to Ham from Boulogne's château-prison and condemned to 'perpetual imprisonment'. Inside he wrote Bonapartist propaganda, helped to edit a *Dictionary of Conversation*, and made love for five years to the daughter of his gaoler. With her help he dressed up as a stonemason and, complete with ladder on his shoulder and a pipe in his mouth, walked out past the guard and made his way to England. He was back in France within three years after the 1848 Revolution.

Ham's church of Notre-Dame in golden stone was built in Romanesque-Gothic style in the twelfth to thirteenth centuries, and altered sympathetically in the seventeenth century.

MARKET Saturday

HOTEL

Valet, 58 rue Noyon (23.81.10.87). ROOMS B–C. MEALS A–D. Shut two weeks in August; 22 December–2 January; Sunday. Restaurant also shut Saturday.

HARDELOT
[Pas-de-Calais]

Hardelot has tried *so* hard to become really fashionable like Le Touquet, 18km S (*see* page 205), but luck has been against it. It was started from scratch as a resort by an Englishman, Sir John Whitley, at the beginning of the twentieth century, because he was impressed by Le Touquet. Its lure was its massive fine sand beach stretching for miles, with considerably more at low tide, meaning that you have quite a little jog to reach the sea. Like Le Touquet, the sands are backed by a pleasant forest.

Hardelot got into the news quickly when a Monsieur Blériot started to use its huge beach for experiments with his aeroplane, then little more than a sand-yacht propelled by a huge sail. Blériot built a villa there and practised flying along the beach. The main hotel was called Hôtel de l'Aviation. But when Blériot finally took off across the Channel in his petrol-engine-driven aeroplane, it was from a beach near Calais and nearer to England.

Whitley bought the castle, which had started life as a defence castle of the Counts of Boulogne. It had been rebuilt several times and finally turned into a pseudo-Gothic, castellated horror in the mid-nineteenth century by an Englishman. Whitley made it into a classy clubhouse for his excellent golf course which soon became fashionable. He made a cricket pitch, too!

Typical seaside villas with little turrets and balconies lined the promenade. The great chef Auguste Escoffier was overlord of hotels and restaurants. The King and Queen of England stayed there twice on holiday, and the King and Queen of Belgium rented a villa. Sand-yacht racing had become fashionable in France and Hardelot was the great centre. In 1914 it was advertising Championships of France and Internationals at its 'Aéroplages', with 'tramways électrique' to Boulogne.

The golf club was the lure between the wars. Then the Germans cleared the promenade to build their West Wall against Allied invasion and covered the dunes and golf course with blockhouses. In 1945 there were six damaged houses and fifty-four blockhouses.

The golf course did not reopen until 1953, the first villas were not built until 1961. Then in 1964 came the apartment blocks. Now there are several big blocks – modern, square, in white concrete and not beautiful, but very comfortable, with balconies overlooking the sea.

Hardelot has taken off in the last few years. A second golf

course puts it in the international grade, and the Golf restaurant is outstanding. It has a good, new modern hotel, the Régina, a country club with superb covered tennis courts and fine swimming-pool, sailing club, sailing and wind-surfing school, sand-yachting. There is plenty of room for many more villas in a sea and forest setting without spoiling it. But it needs more hotels, better restaurants and winter action apart from golf. 'Ripe for development,' as estate agents say.

TOURIST INFORMATION ave Concorde (21.83.51.02)
FESTIVALS End July–early August – Festivals d'Été

HOTELS

Régina, 185 ave François I (21.83.81.88). Comfortable, very quiet, modern. Good cooking and value. ROOMS D–E. MEALS B–F. Shut December, January. Restaurant shut Sunday evening, Monday except in July, August.

Écusson, 443 ave François I (21.83.71.52). ROOMS C–E. MEALS B–E. Shut 10 January–10 February.

RESTAURANT

Golf, 3 ave du Golf (21.83.71.04). Views of the golf course. Sound traditional meals at fair prices. MEALS B–G. Shut 1 February–1 March; 1–11 October; Tuesday evening, Wednesday.

HESDIN
[PAS-DE-CALAIS]

A pleasant, unusual little town with a strange history, Hesdin is at the meeting place of important commercial routes, including the N39 between Montreuil and Arras. See it at nine o'clock on a wet Sunday morning or a wet weekday evening in winter and you would think that it had dropped dead. See it at midday on any day and you realize what a lively, important little place it is.

Its main square, place d'Armes, is delightful, with animated little shops and cafés and a magnificently elegant town hall. Its sumptuously ornate entrance porch and balcony are breath-

Hesdin

taking. Above the porch is the Imperial Eagle of the Hapsburgs. Above the balcony are the royal arms of Spain.

The reason for these coats of arms is that the Hapsburg Emperor Charles V's lands in the north ended at Hesdin, which became in the sixteenth century a highly fortified frontier town between Hapsburg Artois and France. It was especially important as a river crossing. Charles built this town hall as a palace for his sister Marie of Hungary. The palace ballroom is now a theatre.

The palace became a town hall when Artois and Flanders

came under the rule of Philip II of Spain. Charles had been ruler of Spain, the Netherlands and Flanders, as well as most of Germany. While the French were taking Hesdin from the Spanish, their artillery knocked down the town hall's belfry. The present belfry, built in 1857, looks somewhat incongruous.

The market held in the square on Thursday, overspilling into side-streets, is one of the best in northern France.

The sixteenth-century church of Notre-Dame nearby has a notable doorway, too – a Renaissance Arc de Triomphe.

The joy of Hesdin is to wander round its little cobbled side-streets, over little bridges, some hump-backed, crossing the rivulets of the rivers Canche and Ternoise which meet there. If you are a fan of Simenon's Maigret, you might feel that you have been here before. Much of the Maigret TV series, with the late Rupert Davies playing the detective, was shot here.

Hesdin Forest to the N is not large but has delightful forest roads, footpaths and hamlets worth seeing. At the northern edge is Wamin, with a château, just off the D928 leading to Azincourt, where the Battle of Agincourt was fought (*see* page 89). The D108 NW takes you to Lebiez on the Créquoise river and Embry with an arm of the river flowing through and a white church on a hill. Auchy-lès-Hesdin, 5km NE on the D94, has a big paper-mill on what were once monastery grounds where the wounded of Agincourt were treated and an old abbey-church, St Georges, where some of the knights killed at Agincourt are listed and buried. The abbey became a cotton-mill but burned down in 1834. There is a good hotel, Le Monastère.

MARKET Thursday

HOTELS

La Chope, 48 rue d'Arras (21.86.82.73). Our old favourite, grown from Relais Routiers into a comfortable, simple little hotel with Flemish regional and French family cooking. Locals like it. Looks dull from outside: it isn't. ROOMS B–D. MEALS A–E. Shut 23 December–3 January; Friday.

Trois Fontaines, 16 route Abbeville, at Marconne (21.88.81.65). Modern, comfortable, good value but lacks atmosphere. Edge of town. ROOMS D–E. MEALS B–F.

Auberge Monastère, Auchy-lès-Hesdin, 5km NE on the D94,

(21.04.83.54). Good bourgeois cooking. Friendly welcome.
ROOMS C–E. MEALS B–F.

RESTAURANT

Ecurie (*Chez Gaston*) (21.86.86.86). In converted stables as name
implies. Very friendly, big helpings, old-fashioned dishes; used
by businessmen for lunch. MEALS A–D.

HIRSON
[AISNE]

Important rail junction and industrial town making iron, Hirson
is almost on the Belgian border, 18km NE of Vervins and on
N43 between Cambrai and Charleville-Mézières. It is bordered
by very pleasant country, with the Hirson Forest to the north
and St Michel Forest joining it to the north-east. Hirson Forest is
private and has few roads except the D363 which runs over the
Belgian border. A tiny road (Route Verte) off the D963 at the
west end of the forest leads to Étang du Pas Bayard – a lake in a
hole said to be made by the hoof of the legendary horse Bayard
which carried all four of the brothers Aymon, as they escaped
from Charlemagne's men. Around these parts, Charlemagne,
who converted much of western Europe to Christianity at the
point of a sword, is no hero. They did not like the way he
annexed the places and people to his Empire when he had
forcibly converted them.

To reach Étang de Blangy, a smaller forest lake 2km N of
Hirson, you pass under a railway viaduct. The lake has a water-
fall and is in a lovely patch of forest.

St Michel Forest is on hilly ground with trout streams running through. Deer roam among superb oaks, beeches,
hornbeams and pines. It is criss-crossed with forest lanes and
paths marked for walkers. There is an amusement park with a
lake.

The village of St Michel, close to Hirson, is known for its
abbey founded in the tenth century and reconstructed after a
fire in 1715. Its monastic buildings were damaged by another

fire in 1971. The church is almost big enough to be a cathedral (visits by request).

TOURIST INFORMATION rue Guise (shut mornings –
23.58.03.91)
MARKET Monday, Thursday

HOTELS

Hotel Gare, Restaurant Feutry, 86 place Gare, Hirson (23.58.16.45). Station hotel run by a wine merchant and French Master of Wine. Simple rooms. Delightful low-priced meals. ROOMS A–B. MEALS A–D. Shut part of February; Monday.
Domaine du Tilleul, Landouzy, 7km SW of Hirson by the D963, D36, (23.98.48.00). Beside a river in big tranquil park. Chef from Maxim's, Paris. ROOMS E–G. MEALS C–F.

HONDSCHOOTE
[NORD]

Centre of flax country where until the seventeenth century they made a very light serge in 3000 workshops. Now one or two factories ret and scutch flax – that is, they treat the stem to take its fibre which is then sent in skeins to the spinning factories around Lille or exported to make linen.

The flax growing in the fields is tender green in early spring. In early summer it breaks into a pretty blue or a white flower for a very short time. Then it is cut and lies in the fields until it goes reddy brown. The seed is used for linseed oil, the central fibre for linen.

Hondschoote is near the Colme canal SE of Dunkerque and very near the Belgian border. The canal continues to Bergues and is joined there by the canal from Dunkerque. The waterways to the N around the village of Les Moëres were marshes which were drained in the seventeenth century, flooded again from 1645–1746, and again flooded by the French in 1940 to hold off the German tank advance during the Dunkerque evacuation.

The sixteenth-century Gothic-Renaissance-style town hall is

one of the finest in the north. It is beautiful inside, too. You can see a great tableau of the Battle of Hondschoote in 1793 when the French army under Houchard defeated Austrian and English troops commanded by that famous Grand Old Duke of York, liberating Dunkerque from a siege and saving French Flanders from invasion.

Next to it is an inn dating from 1617. St Vaast's church has a slender spire 82 metres high, built in the sixteenth century. It is all that has survived a fire which ravaged the town in 1582.

500 metres north of the town is a windmill (Nordmeulen) which was built in 1127 and is claimed to be the oldest in Europe. A miller restored it after the Second World War and kept it working until 1959.

MARKET Friday morning
FESTIVALS Mid-June – Brocante (secondhand street
fair); first week in September – Karyole Feest
(agricultural fair)

LE HOURDEL
[*See* Cayeux-sur-Mer, page 110]

LÉCLUSE
[*See* Arleux, page 84]

HUCQUELIERS
[PAS-DE-CALAIS]

An agricultural village on the D343 road SE from Desvres. This road goes through very pleasant countryside but few people exploring this charming area take it because they prefer the D127 in the valley of the Course a few kilometres W. Hucqueliers is not a pretty place at all, but it has atmosphere as a typical little farming centre to which farm families come for simple shopping, to service their vehicles and farm machinery, to meet at the inn and for the odd meal out. There are some seventeenth-century houses, and a fifteenth-century church which was opposite a château destroyed in the time of Louis XIV. Louis, who was broke, and his minister, Mazarin, had placed a heavy new tax on the people of the Boulonnais for guarding their frontier against the Spanish to the north. The peasants of Hucqueliers, Marquise and Desvres revolted. 3000 shut themselves in the château at Hucqueliers. Afraid that the rebellion would spread, the lieutenant of Picardie, the Marquis de Montpezat, brought up cannons, fired, and shot a lump out of the castle. His men captured 586 peasants. The leaders were executed; Porlet du Clivet, the main leader, was flayed alive and most of the rest were sent to the terrible galleys.

There are still many old farmhouses in the surrounding countryside.

From Hucqueliers you can take the little D148 W to join the D127 at a trout farm.

RESTAURANT

Cocatrix, Grand'Place (21.90.51.61). A local institution. The simple inn where the village meets and eats. Good value. MEALS A–C.

LAON
[AISNE]

When it was little known to tourists in the 1950s, Laon was one of my favourite cities in France. I still like it now that it is almost *too* well known, but it is one of those old cities with narrow streets which does not take well to much traffic.

The old town with ramparts and ancient gateways was built on a site so perfect for defence that in the eighth to tenth centuries it was actually the capital of France when Paris was a village. Charlemagne's mother Berthe Au Grand Pied (Bertha of the Big Feet) made it her seat. Hugues Capet, elected King in 987, moved his Government to Paris.

Cathedral at Laon

The old part of Laon stands on a steep hill with the newer town on the plain below. As you enter the town you see tree-lined boulevards rising steeply to the old walls of the fortified medieval town, which clusters in narrow streets around the superb twelfth-century cathedral. This is one of the oldest and finest Gothic churches in Europe. It has impeccable symmetry – a strong but gentle church. The early-Gothic style was, above all, seeking space, height and light. The main façade is truly splendid. The 43-metre-high lantern tower is rather a Romanesque-style leftover, but blends very well. The two flanking towers, 51 metres tall, pierced and turreted, have been called the most beautiful in the world. At the corners are big oxen, put there in memory of the sturdy beasts which dragged the stone up that punishing hill. The effect of the nave and long choir, flanked by large arches on heavy cylindrical pillars, leading to the beautiful rose window and bays with thirteenth-century glass, is beautiful and awesome.

From the thirteenth-century ramparts, views SE stretch far to the plain of Champagne.

Another church, St Martin, was built with an abbey in the twelfth century and altered in the thirteenth. It was restored after the Second World War. Next to it are abbey buildings of the sixteenth to seventeenth centuries.

TOURIST INFORMATION place Parvis (23.20.28.62)
MARKETS Tuesday, Wednesday morning, Thursday,
Saturday afternoon

HOTEL
Bannière de France, 11 rue Franklin-Roosevelt (23.23.21.44). Old posting inn in the medieval town. Very pleasant. Good old-style cooking. Gets very full, so book. ROOMS C–E. MEALS C–F. Shut 20 December–15 January.

RESTAURANT
Petite Auberge, 45 boul. Brossolette (23.23.02.38). Interesting dishes, some spicy. Pricey. MEALS B (weekdays), D–G. Shut Saturday lunch, Sunday evening.

LENS
[PAS-DE-CALAIS]

One of the old coal-mining towns of northern France, surrounded for years by shale heaps and old, dirty-brick miners' houses, it was almost totally destroyed and its mines flooded by the Germans in the First World War, badly damaged in the Second World War, only to be hit by the near-total collapse of coal-mining from the 1960s, after which it lost 5000 of its 42,000 inhabitants in ten years. The last pit closed in December 1990. It has built a new modern industrial zone, a zone for artisans, and a sports stadium where the town's renowned football team, Racing Club de Lens, plays. It has a technical university institute.

Lens is 18km SE of Béthune and the two were part of the same canton until 1962. The A26 and A21 motorways meet 9km to the W, the A21 and A1 9km to the E.

MARKETS Tuesday, Friday
FESTIVAL Last Sunday in June – Grande Fête

LICQUES
[PAS-DE-CALAIS]

To the French, Licques, the little town off the main roads 23km NE of Boulogne, means chickens, to which turkeys have been added recently. Licques chickens are named on the menus of the best restaurants in France. Most of the Licques turkeys are exported to Britain. There is a big turkey fair with a Festival de la Dinde (Turkey Festival) on the last two Mondays before Christmas. The chickens are sold at the Monday market throughout the year.

The best way to drive to Licques from Boulogne is to turn off the N42 to the charming village of Le Wast (*see* page 214), take the D127 N to Hardinghen, then right on to the pretty D191 into Licques, a green, hilly route. Licques still has eighteenth-century buildings, including its old abbey church, town hall and school. The town stands beneath a hill 165 metres high, with views over the Hem river valley.

To me Licques is a rather sad symbol of changing France. In the early 1950s I was in the village inn with the Gaulliste Deputy, who lived opposite, drinking a bottle of champagne which he had offered, when the innkeeper suggested that he should go to the local trout farm to get fresh trout for our lunch. He returned with a man in blue overalls, hands covered in oil, who sat down with us. He was from the old, scruffy garage next door. He bantered with the Deputy heartily and mercilessly, and insisted upon buying us another bottle of champagne. Then he left, to return when the trout in almonds was ready, dressed in a clean shirt and trousers. He joined us for lunch. He was the Mayor – a Communist.

I did not return to Licques for some years. The inn was tarted up and almost empty. The garage next door was modern and I was served by a smart young man with clean hands, in clean white overalls. The petrol pump, of course, was now electric – not one of those nice hand-operated models the Communist Mayor had used. The only thing the same was my old Lagonda, with 164,000 miles on the clock.

MARKETS Monday; last two Mondays before Christmas – Turkey Fair

LIESSIES
[NORD]

In the valley of the Helpe river, near Eppe-Sauvage (*see* page 131) and Val Joly, the lake for watersports, and E of Avesnes-sur-Helpe. Its sixteenth-century church has some fine artefacts and goldsmiths' work from a former abbey S of the village.

Château de la Motte, a very impressive eighteenth-century château in rose brick, is reached to the S by a road alongside the Étang de Vieille Forge. It is mirrored in the water of another lake. Once a rest home for old monks, it is now a hotel. It is on the edge of the Val Joly Forest, which has pleasant forest roads and walks. The D963 runs through it to Trélon and continues through attractive scenery to Hirson (*see* page 152).

HOTEL
Château de la Motte (27.61.81.94). See text. Run down – certainly no Relais et Châteaux hotel. But in lovely parkland and peaceful. Meals for residents only or by advance order. ROOMS B–D. MEALS A–E. Shut 20 December–31 January.

See also Locquignol, page 161, 8km NW of Liessies.

LIGNY-HAUCOURT
[NORD]

10km SE of Cambrai, also called Ligny-en-Cambrésis, hamlet
with a château dating from the thirteenth century which is now a
hotel. The thirteenth-century part is the round bell tower with a
six-sided pointed roof. The rest was built in the fifteenth century
in Flemish Renaissance style. It is built round a courtyard and
has a garden and a small park with fallow deer inside its walls.
The moat has been filled in. Beyond the walls are the village
houses and church. The old armoury is now the hotel's dining-
room, with a large stone fireplace. Through a grille in the floor
you can see a tunnel, now lit up. It is something of a mystery,
and may have been a dungeon for prisoners. In 1917 occupying
Germans discovered firing steps used by archers and later
walled up, and in the cellars graffiti and coats of arms.

HOTEL

Château de Ligny (27.85.25.84). See text. Only nine rooms, which
are pricey. Evening meals expensive. ROOMS G. MEALS C–G
(lunch), G (evening). Shut 2 January–15 February. Restaurant
shut Saturday lunch, Monday.

LILLE
[*See* Major Towns, page 59]

LILLERS
[PAS-DE-CALAIS]

On the river Nave and N43, 13km NW of Béthune, Lillers is a
small industrial town known for the most complete Romanesque
building in the north of France and for a very important sugar
cooperative refining sugar beet grown in a large area around it.

The Collegiate church of St Omer was built between 1120
and 1150 and altered somewhat in the seventeenth century. The

inside is still remarkable. It is light and broad. The three-storeyed nave with a wooden ceiling is beautiful. Its façade has suffered with time, especially during the First World War. In 1985 the Anglo-Norman south façade was re-made after caving in during a service in 1971.

Lillers now has plastic and metallic industries.

LOCQUIGNOL
[NORD]

Mormal Forest, covering 9,105 hectares 20km SE of Valenciennes, W of the Sambre river, is the biggest in northern France. It has now recovered from mass felling of trees by the Germans in the First World War. It covers high ground and slopes with high-quality beech and oak, and in the NE some 200-year-old trees have survived. It has 55km of forest routes, car-parks, picnic spots and a little lake. Roe deer hide by hidden streams and tranquil glades which make walking through it a joy. Right in the middle, on the little D33, which runs through the forest from Le Quesnoy to Berlaimont, is Locquignol, its biggest hamlet with 320 inhabitants and two inns. Lovely centre for a walking holiday.

HOTELS

Hostellerie La Touraille (27.34.21.21). Charming inn full of old-fashioned lace and frills, and snow-white cottons. Very romantic. Very nice meals. ROOMS D–G. MEALS C–G. Shut December, January except Christmas, New Year; Sunday evening, Monday.

Forestière, 18 route Le Quesnoy (27.34.20.18). Simple, single-storey auberge in forest near to village, with four rooms. Nice bourgeoise regional cooking. ROOMS B–C. MEALS B–F. Shut Tuesday.

LONG
[Somme]

Pretty village on a hill beside the Somme between Amiens and Abbeville, with a series of small lakes across the river. Its castle, in a lovely position overlooking the river, is a wonderful example of Louis XV architecture in pink brick and white stone (open 20 August to 30 September). Its great church, built in the nineteenth century in Gothic style, has a prized organ.

LONGPONT
[Aisne]

11km NE of Villers-Cotterets and 13km SW of Soissons. St Louis (King Louis IX of France) attended the consecration of the abbey in 1227. Now it is a rather lovely ruin. The thirteenth-century storehouse was turned into a château, rebuilt in the eighteenth century and restored after 1918 (open daily except Thursday, 1 March to 31 October; open Saturday, Sunday 1 November to end February). The village church has some interesting fourteenth-century painted panels.

HOTEL
Abbaye, rue Tourelles (23.96.02.44). Forest views. Logis de France. Rooms C–E. Meals C–F.

LONGPRÉ-LES-CORPS-SAINTS
[Somme]

This impressively named village stands in the Somme valley on the D3, the Abbeville-Amiens road. There are small lakes beside it, and across the river is the road to Long (*see* above).

Its splendid name came from relics brought home by a local lord from the Crusades, and they are still on show in the choir of the church.

Rommel's 7th Panzer Division crossed the Somme near here in 1940 on a railway bridge which had not been blown up. The French General Weygand had been hoping to hold the Somme as the French and English had done in the First World War. Longpré was almost wiped out in the fighting. There is a big French cemetery 2km SE at Condé-Folie.

LUCHEUX
[SOMME]

A little village 6½km NE of Doullens just N of the Arras–Doullens road, the N25. In a pleasant woodland setting, it is worth seeing for its Romanesque church with amusing decorations and the partly restored château on a hill.

The church capitals show light-hearted scenes portraying the Seven Deadly Sins.

In the keep of the castle St Joan was imprisoned after her capture at Compiègne before being moved to Le Crotoy and then Rouen. The castle was built by the Counts of St Pol between the twelfth and sixteenth centuries. You can see the thirteenth-century Hall of Justice. In the village is a twelfth-century gate tower.

LUMBRES
[PAS-DE-CALAIS]

A little town just off the N42, 12km before St Omer driving from Boulogne, it has a paper-mill and a small cement works, and frankly you would not bother to stop but for two treasures it hides. The first is Manoir d'Acquembronne, which is in the hamlet of Liauwette on the edge of the town – a handsome fifteenth-century manor house with two towers on a magnificent site. The second is Moulin de Mombreux, an attractive old water-mill on the little river Bléquin, a tributary of the river Aa which runs through Lumbres. Mombreux has been a superb

Moulin de Mombreux

little hotel and restaurant since Jean-Marc Gaudry came here from L'Oasis, the three-star Michelin restaurant in Napoule, about twenty-five years ago. I was lucky enough to be one of his first customers. I had a splendid meal and have been having splendid meals ever since. The little river runs past on grassy banks and now, at the bottom of the garden, there are delightfully comfortable bedrooms in an extension which arches over the river and fits in perfectly well with the mill.

Trout fisheries have been set up recently by the river Aa – extraordinary to people who saw it polluted by the paper-mills. Paper was made here from the fifteenth century. Modern purification plants have worked miraculously. The Aa is clear and alive.

A good place to fish is the village of Nielles-lès-Bléquin, 5km SW, with a lake as well as the Bléquin river.

HOTEL

Moulin de Mombreux, route de Bayenghem (21.39.62.44). See text. Expensive but well worth it. ROOMS G. MEALS F–G. Shut 21–29 December.

MALO-LES-BAINS
[*See* Dunquerque, page 54]

MAROILLES
[NORD]

12km W of Avesnes-sur-Helpe and near the fine Mormal Forest, Maroilles is known for its two cheeses called Maroilles and Le Dauphin, originally produced at a Benedictine abbey of which a few seventeenth-century buildings remain. Maroilles cheese was invented in the tenth century and has a mighty powerful smell and taste. It is creamy coloured and soaked in brine or beer. In Flanders it is sometimes called *puant* (stinking). In the area it is made into *goyère au Maroilles* – a cheese tart, with equal quantities of this cheese and *fromage blanc* (soft cream cheese).

Dauphin cheese has a strong smell, too. It is soft, smooth and flavoured with herbs. It is usually crescent- or heart-shaped and is rather similar to boulette d'Avesnes.

MAUBEUGE
[NORD]

Maubeuge's Beer Festival in July lasts twelve days! This important industrial town on the N49 between Bavay and the Belgian border used to manufacture arms but was almost burned down by German incendiary bombs in 1940 and has been reborn, modern and white. The river Sambre runs through it, and the industrial section is on both sides of it. To the N is the beautiful Porte de Mons, built in 1685, part of Vauban's fortifications which included a system of outer forts behind which 40,000 people could shelter. Now the remains shelter pleasant gardens.

The church of St Pierre was rebuilt after the Second World War to the design of André Lurçat, and is a very interesting piece of modern religious architecture. Its porch is ornamented with a fine mosaic by his more famous kinsman, Jean Lurçat, master of ceramics as well as tapestries. The impressive church belltower of glass slabs has a carillon of twenty-eight bells which give unusually enjoyable concerts at noon on the first Sunday of each month.

The seventeenth-century chapter house of the lay canonesses, called Les Dames de Maubeuge, now contains a museum which is mostly of local history and ceramics, but with paintings which include works by Van Dyck and one of the Coypel family.

TOURIST INFORMATION 1 porte de Bavay, ave du Parc
(27.62.11.93)
MARKETS Sunday, Monday, Wednesday, Saturday
FESTIVALS April – Carnival Procession; first and second
weeks July – Beer Festival

HOTEL
Grand Hotel, Paris Restaurant, 1 porte de Paris (27.64.63.16). Good modern Logis with a wide choice of menus, specializing enthusiastically in Flemish cooking. ROOMS C–E. MEALS C–G.

MERLIMONT
[PAS-DE-CALAIS]

Bathing beach just S of Le Touquet with the main village 3km inland on the D940, it has become renowned in recent years for its great amusement park, La Bagatelle, which lures families to drive from Paris in summer.

The original Merlimont village was buried in sand in the fifteenth century. It grew up in its present position around 1770, and the little beach resort Merlimont Plage was started in 1900.

La Bagatelle was set up after the Second World War in the grounds of a big house called Château St Hubert which had been built in the 1930s by a rich Yorkshire wool broker – allegedly as a bolt-hole to take a girlfriend. It had been used in the Second World War as an officers' mess for the German fighter pilots using the little airfield on the edge of the estate. Now the pleasure park is known over most of France.

It covers 24 hectares, has 150 attractions from miniature train rides to go-karts, monorail, roller-coaster and boating lake, snack bars and restaurants. The zoo has over 400 animals and birds. After you have paid an entrance fee, most of the attractions are free. You pay extra for some things such as the ghost train, big wheel and boat hire. It is open early March to late October. It has a good campsite, St Hubert (four-star).

MONTCAVREL
[PAS-DE-CALAIS]

The hamlet of Montcavrel where the D151 meets the D150 between Estrée and Hucqueliers, N of Montreuil, used to be so important that its lords, the Monchy family, then the Mailly, were among the grandest in Picardie. Its fifteenth-century church of St Quentin is in Flamboyant style. The woods further along the D150 past Recques are the remains of Montcavrel Forest.

There are three châteaux. The Renaissance-style Château d'Hérambault was, in fact, built in 1845. From the D149 you can see Château de Montechor, which belonged to the Monchy family until 1800. Of Montcavrel Château itself only two towers remain. In 1717 Peter the Great, Tsar of all the Russias, the man who built Leningrad and the Russian navy, stayed there on his way from Calais to Paris.

MONTREUIL
[Pas-de-Calais]

Montreuil has been an even more delightful place in recent times since a new stretch of the N1 was built at the bottom of the hill to bypass it, instead of running through its medieval streets as the old route did when I first stayed there. Not that Montreuil has become a museum town. It is a lively little place where people come from villages far and wide to do their household shopping, to meet in cafés, and above all to go to the Saturday market. They buy their medicines, their gardening tools, books and magazines, their crockery and cutlery there. This old, walled medieval town really grows on you.

Until very recently it was still called Montreuil-sur-Mer. In the Middle Ages the river Canche was wide and navigable and joined its harbour to the sea, which was then very much nearer. It was an important port with 10,000 people, compared with 2700 now. It had eight churches.

The port itself, down the hill where the market stands, was called Poulie. The great castle on the hill and the ramparts were built by King Philippe Auguste, rival of Richard Coeur de Lion, in 1186. Montreuil-sur-Mer's rival the over the centuries was Rye, one of Cinque Ports in Sussex. The sailors of each attacked each other's ships and raided each other's towns, looting, sacking and burning. Between times, they got together to smuggle.

Like Rye, Montreuil has not actually been 'sur Mer' for centuries. Rye, at least, still has a harbour with fishing boats and pleasure craft coming in and out. The Canche at Montreuil is a trout stream.

In 1537 the Hapsburg Emperor Charles V and English troops of Henry VIII took the town, pillaged and burned it. Charles had the harbour filled in. Montreuil lost its trade. Many of the people moved to Abbeville. Montreuil slept until Napoleon planned his invasion of Britain from Boulogne in 1803, when his commanders Soult and Ney stayed there with their personal staffs.

In the First World War, General Douglas Haig, British Commander-in-Chief, set up his headquarters from March 1916 to April 1919 at the Château de Beaurepaire, 4km out of Montreuil on the D138 near Saint-Nicolas. Some 5000 British troops were based in Montreuil. There must have been even more English spoken in the great square than there is now on a fine weekend in summer.

The bronze statue of Haig on a horse stands just off the main square in front of the early nineteenth-century theatre. Somewhere on the outskirts of Montreuil the British had vast dog kennels run by the Royal Army Veterinary Corps. There were 200 dogs, each in its own kennel, lined up with military precision. They were used as message carriers and guard dogs in the front line. The noise must have been awesome!

The first thing to do when exploring Montreuil is to see the remains of the château and to walk the ramparts. It is signposted as La Citadelle and the way in is across the green from Hotel Château de Montreuil, which is in Chaussée des Capucins. The château is shut on Tuesday, but you can climb to the ramparts from many places around the old town on the hill by little paths. Walking the ramparts on grass paths takes anything from thirty-five to sixty minutes according to how long you spend admiring the views over the farmlands, the Canche valley, the old roofs of the town and the monastery of Notre-Dame des Prés in the valley. Do at least walk *some* of it to see the views.

The château itself still has its porch entrance, two great entrance towers, its chapel and arsenal. Inside are the coats of arms of local knights who rode out from here to die fighting England's Henry V at Agincourt. It's a formidable list.

In the narrow streets below, many of them still cobbled, are many ancient houses and little shops, with lovely old buildings such as the old monastery church of St Saulve, built in the twelfth century, altered several times but still beautiful, with a magnificent Flamboyant nave. It contains treasure from St Austreberthe Abbey, including a fine wooden cross covered with silver strips (seventh to eighth centuries).

Chapelle de l'Hôtel-Dieu nearby, on the corner of place Gambetta, where the post office stands and where you can usually park, was a tower built in 1200, which now contains a beautiful Flamboyant-Gothic chapel. It was reconstructed in 1875 by the architect Claude Norman, a pupil of Viollet-le-Duc who himself reconstructed the medieval city of Carcassonne, and restored Notre-Dame in Paris. Inside it has some superb carved panelling and furnishings, including a fine Baroque altar surround. The lacy stonework of its entrance porch is lovely.

Many old buildings have changed their use. The chapel of St Austreberthe Abbey is part of the *lycée* (the senior school), and the Carmelite church houses the Industrial Tribunal. The ancient orphanage is a nursery school and library. The police station (*sous-préfecture*) is in a beautiful mansion built in 1742.

The old inn called La France, with a separate restaurant called Relais du Roy, that faces the main road from the upper town to the market square (rue Pierre Ledente) used to be a famous posting inn where the Paris *diligence* (stage-coach) stopped. It was called Le Roy (the King) before the Revolution, La France after it.

Many years ago, when it was in a state of utter post-war decay, I walked along its corridors, past empty rooms and a toilet with a suite of ornate nineteenth-century cast iron with a flowery motif and chattering pipes, to my huge bedroom over-looking the courtyard. Down there one wall was covered with a massive mural, flaking badly, showing an eighteenth-century gentleman stepping into a post-chaise, surrounded by little ragged children holding out their hands. It was of the Yorkshire parson, the author Laurence Sterne, starting his *Sentimental Journey Through France and Italy* by distributing *sous* to the poor.

'They order these things better in France,' he wrote. And generations have used the phrase to refer to hotels and meals. In fact, he was talking about begging. I returned recently to a much smaller but much nicer bedroom with its own little bathroom. The mural has been repainted and heavily varnished over. It is very amateurish, in garish colours. The tea room where coach tourists following in Sterne's footsteps (or wheel tracks) were refreshed is obviously used now for local functions. I wondered how many modern visitors have read Sterne – or even heard of him.

They *have* heard of Victor Hugo's *Les Misérables*, of course, in which the ex-villain Jean Valjean, purged by good works and a life of sacrifice, and a respected Mayor of Montreuil, learns that an innocent man is being tried for his crimes and faces death. The locals say that Valjean is the most famous mayor the town has produced!

Hotel Château de Montreuil isn't a château at all but an English-looking country house, built by an Englishman at the beginning of the century, in a very English-looking garden. It is a hotel owned by one of the best young chefs in France, Christian Germain, and his delightful English wife, Lindsay. Christian worked at the old Montcalm restaurant in Westerham, Kent, then as Chef de Cuisine for the Roux brothers at the Michelin three-star Waterside Inn at Bray. I tried to learn a few tricks by working in his Montreuil kitchen for a week. I invented the straight croissant – mine just would not stay curved! And he accused me, of all people, of being too light-handed with the Grand Marnier in the soufflé. A terrible insult! My bolognese sauce has enough wine in it to deserve an appellation contrôlée and people have been known to sniff my soups, raise the bowl and say, 'Gentlemen – the Queen!'

The hotel was used as a German anti-invasion headquarters in 1944. In the loft there is still a notice ordering troops to 'salute the Führer before entering'. I prefer to bow to the chef.

TOURIST INFORMATION place Poissonerie (midsummer – 21.06.04.27); town hall (low season – 21.06.01.33)
MARKET Saturday

HOTELS

Château de Montreuil (21.81.53.04). See text. Relais et Château hotel. Pricey, but worth every franc. Extra rooms added, beautifully decorated. ROOMS F–G. MEALS G. Shut 15 December– early February; Thursday lunch except in July, August.
Bellevue, ave 11 November (21.06.04.19). Out of town, down by the station. Rooms improved. Meals excellent value. ROOMS D–E. MEALS A–E. Shut 15–29 December.

RESTAURANTS

Darnetal, place Darnetal (21.06.04.87). In a little square with fountain and trees. Six simple bedrooms usually booked well ahead. One of my favourite haunts since Robert Bureau opened it twenty years ago. Alas, the effervescent Robert has retired, so some delightful eccentricity is lost, but not friendliness, service or value, for his loyal, still-young chef and charming wife have taken over. Old-style dishes of fresh food very nicely cooked. ROOMS B–D. MEALS B–E. Shut part January, part October; Tuesday (check by phone), Monday evening.

Grenouillère, at La Madelaine, 3km SW by D917, D139 (21.06.07.22). Old farm alongside river Canche. Four improved bedrooms. I have known it for thirty years and the funny frogs on the wall are still overeating to bursting point. Excellent young chef. High prices, especially for wine. ROOMS F–G. MEALS F–G. Shut 15 December–15 January; Tuesday evening, Wednesday except in July, August.

NAOURS
[SOMME]

30 metres beneath the old village of Naours, 20km N of Amiens, W of the N25, is a little underground 'town' which was built up over centuries, all dug out by man.

When the Barbarian invasions came to France in the third and fourth centuries, and again when the Norsemen raided almost every year in the eighth and ninth centuries, looting, burning, killing, raping and taking people into slavery, the people living here dug out a great bolt-hole. As invaders approached they went to earth, taking with them cattle and supplies. They made air-holes, dug wells, baked bread and spun wool. In the Hundred Years War, the Wars of Religion and the Thirty Years War they extended the total length of thirty galleries to 3000 metres – about 3km. They had stables, cow sheds, a blacksmith's shop, a three-nave chapel and a statue of the Virgin. There were 300 chambers, roads, and space for 3000 people to work and live.

The caves were either forgotten or, as in other places, people became frightened of them because of local legends about haunting and evil. They were used by contrabanders of salt in the eighteenth century when the salt tax was so harsh that it was causing great hunger among poorer people. Salt was vital in those days before refrigeration or tinning to keep meat and vegetables for the winter.

In 1887 Abbé Danicourt, the local curé, found documents about the caves and explored them. In 1905, twenty gold pieces were found of the fifteenth, sixteenth and seventeenth centuries.

In 1943, the Germans took over the underground town for their army and Field-Marshal Rommel had a headquarters there in 1943 until June 1944. Now there is an interesting but small museum of old trades in them with guided tours (15–January to 15 November). Above is an amusement park and on a spur two lovely old windmills rebuilt there.

NEUVILLE-SOUS-MONTREUIL
[PAS-DE-CALAIS]

A surprising village just off the N39 below Montreuil. It may sound like a modern industrial suburb, but it was founded in the eleventh century, built alongside water-meadows on the right bank of the Canche, and is an attractive old village.

Much of it belonged to the monastery, Chartreuse de Notre-Dame des Prés and its farm Basse Cour. It was founded in 1328 by disciples of St Bruno and became very rich and renowned until ravaged by the English, then the Protestants in wars. Louis XIV revitalized it by giving special privileges, but it was sold after the Revolution and pulled down to make stables and barns for local peasants. The monks came back in 1870 to a superb new building designed by Claude Normand, and they bought back the farm. But they had to leave in 1901 when the State separated entirely from the Church. A local benefactor, Dr Victor Morel, turned it into a hospice attached to the well-known hospital at Campagne-des-Hedins, which he founded. It is a superb building which you can see from the ramparts at Montreuil (*see* page 168).

NOYON
[OISE]

Charlemagne, who built an Empire at swordpoint in the name of Christianity, was crowned King of Neustria (Normandy) there in 768. Hugues Capet, founder of a dynasty of kings, was crowned King of France there in 987.

Noyon was a bishopric by 581, combined with Tournai, and its great ancient cathedral still dominates the thriving industrial town.

At the meeting of the Oise river and two canals, Noyon is 24km NE of Compiègne by the N32 and is alongside attractive forests. In fact, you can drive to Compiègne on very pleasant roads through the Ourscamps, Laigue and Compiègne Forests. And although Noyon has heavy traffic, it is a pleasant town because it was rebuilt in old style after heavy damage in the First World War. The cathedral had extensive repairs, as did the fine semicircle of houses in Grande Place.

The cathedral was started in the twelfth century, the fifth church to be built on the same site, and finished at the end of the thirteenth century. It is not *quite* finished, for the two heavy square towers on the façade, one thirteenth, the other four-teenth century, were intended to be topped by spires. Neverthe-less, the cathedral shows the first blossoming of soaring Gothic splendour which was emerging from sober Romanesque.

The chapter house and the cloister, which has fine arcades, are thirteenth century. The sixteenth-century half-timbered chapter library has 3000 volumes, including a ninth-century manuscript *Évangéliaire* with gorgeous illuminations (decorative illustrations).

The puritanical Jean Calvin (1509–64), who did so much to promote early Protestantism, was born in Noyon in 1509, and his birthplace, as well as the fifteenth century town hall, was reconstructed to original plans after war destruction. Calvin's house is a museum which includes sixteenth-century Bibles in French, many of which lost their covers when buried to avoid discovery, and his 'Chaire de Désert', the pulpit from which he preached sermons when travelling through the countryside (shut Tuesday).

The romantic ruins of the old Cistercian abbey of Ourscamps are in a lovely woodland setting. Built in the twelfth to thirteenth centuries, the abbey was partly destroyed in the Revolution, used as a factory, and sacked and burned by the Germans in the First World War; enough survived to be occupied by a religious order, however. The old infirmary, a splendid thirteenth-century monastic hall, is now the chapel (open to visitors).

TOURIST INFORMATION Town Hall (44.44.21.88)

FESTIVAL Early July – Fête des Fruits Rouges

HOTELS

St Eloi, 81 boul. Carnot (44.44.01.49). Eighteenth-century house totally renovated. ROOMS B–D. MEALS A–D. Shut 20 December–4 January. Restaurant shut Wednesday evening.

RESTAURANT

Dame Journe, 2 boul. Mony (44.44.01.33). Outstanding value. MEALS A–E. Shut 15–21 August; 31 December–6 January; Monday and Sunday evenings.

OFFOY
[SOMME]

Domaine des Îles (6km from Ham by the D330 and D17). Flower and amusement park with lakes, train-rides, rowing, pedalos, pony-rides, cycling, boating. A day's fishing. Free amusement park (swings etc.). Restaurant. Open daily 1 April to 30 September. Flower park open 1 March to 30 October (tel. 22.60.93.50).

OYE-PLAGE
[PAS-DE-CALAIS]

14km E of Calais by the D119 and spreading to the N1, this town used to be on the sea when the Norsemen liked to land here in

the ninth century to see what they could pick up in the way of
loot and women, and in 1164, when Thomas à Becket fled here
from Canterbury during one of his arguments with Henry II of
England. The sea has receded 2km but the sands and dunes
spread for 11km and just about reach Grand Fort-Philippe at
Gravelines. There is a long promenade. It was named for the
wild geese (*oie*) which used to invade here in the Middle Ages.
Now known for shellfish. There are nine campsites nearby and a
small bathing resort is planned.

HOTEL

Abri Cotier, ave Plage, Hutters de Oye-Plage (21.35.80.43). Ori-
ginally advertised as the only 'motel à l'américaine' in the north.
Separate bungalows. Now known for seafood. ROOMS D–E.
MEALS C–G. Shut October (check by phone).

PÉRONNE
[SOMME]

Poor Péronne seems to have survived very well considering its
troubles, for even by Somme standards it took a terrifying bat-
tering in the First World War. It is at the meeting of the Somme
and Cologne rivers, near where the Nord canal joins, between
Amiens and St Quentin. Its character is made by the pools and
marshlands around it, called *hardines* and rather similar to the
hortillonnages waterways around Amiens (*see* page 29). They produce the renowned *anguilles* (eels), which are made into a pâté or
are smoked, and pike, made into pike *quenelles*. The commercial
port on the Nord canal is shared by pleasure boats these days.

Four great circular towers of the historic thirteenth-century
castle have been rebuilt and are enclosed in a colossal
seventeenth-century brick bastion. Of the town walls Porte de
Bretagne (1602) is still there with its drawbridge and outer
defences.

It was in this castle that Louis XI of France was imprisoned
in 1468 by Charles le Téméraire, Charles the Bold, Duke of
Burgundy.

The French and Burgundians were arguing over Picardie. Louis was invited to meet Charles in Péronne to try to settle the matter. Charles imprisoned Louis in the castle at Péronne and forced him to sign the humiliating Treaty of Péronne under which he denounced his allies in Flanders who were revolting against Charles. Sir Walter Scott described the scene graphically in his novel *Quentin Durward*. France got Péronne back but it took a local heroine to hold it when the Spanish under Charles V attacked it from their Flanders territories in 1536. A woman called Marie Fourré personally killed a Spaniard and galvanized the local men into resistance, ending the siege.

Wellington took it from Napoleon's forces in 1815 in his memorable march towards Paris. It was bombarded by the Prussians for thirteen days in 1870 in the Franco-Prussian War. The Germans made it into one of their strongpoints in 1914, turned it into a base and developed a formidable fortress up a hill, Mont-Saint-Quentin, 2km N, which the French failed to take in the Allied 1916 offensive. It was the Australians who took both the hill and Péronne in 1918, but the fighting was so tough that the town was laid waste and completely destroyed.

TOURIST INFORMATION 31 rue St Fursy (afternoons – 22.84.42.38)

MARKET Friday (fish), Saturday

HOTEL

Remparts, 21 rue Beaubois (22.84.01.22). Attractive, with flowers, coloured blinds. Rooms vary. Classic cooking in a medieval-style dining-room. Local smoked eels, *quennelles de brochet*. ROOMS B–E. MEALS A–F. Restaurant shut 4–13 August.

PICQUIGNY
[SOMME]

Built between the fourteenth and seventeenth centuries, the castle at Picquigny overlooking the Somme 13km W of Amiens must have been a very formidable fortress. Even the ruins are most impressive.

It was built above a most important crossing of the Somme, to defend the bridge. The French stopped Edward III of England and his Army from crossing it in 1346. The Burgundians burned the town and castle but it was restored by Louis XI who built a new bridge. And there on the isle of Trève in the centre of the Somme in 1475 Louis XI and Edward IV of England signed the very important Treaty of Picquigny which effectively ended the Hundred Years War. Although the English had been driven out of everywhere except Calais, the embers were still smouldering under the ashes.

Louis XI believed that every man had his price. He paid 10,000 écus a month to his physician to keep him alive – wise in those days. Believing that the English were 'inclined towards war against this kingdom', and fearing an alliance between them and Burgundy, he bought them off at Picquigny, giving 50,000 écus to Edward, 16,000 écus to his Ministers, and other gifts. He even humbled himself to suggest that Edward should call himself 'King of France' and Louis should be 'Prince Louis'.

But they mistrusted each other so much that they met to make peace in a specially built hut with bars separating them – like caged lions, wrote the historian Commynes.

Louis XI rarely kept his promises or treaties. Captured by the Duke of Burgundy at Péronne, he promised everything, then denied the whole thing once he was free. He said: 'He who has success has honour.' To imprison those who disagreed with him, he built appalling cages which swung from a roof and were too small for a man to stretch out. He was so frightened of reprisals in his old age that he lived and died shut up in a castle at Plessis-les-Tours, surrounded by archers, men-at-arms and the bodies of men he distrusted hanging from the trees outside. They called it Louis' Orchard. England's Edward IV, a handsome, licentious man, spent his life fighting Henry VI for the crown of England in the civil War of the Roses between his House of York and the rival House of Lancaster, and was just as quick to execute his enemies.

Later, Picquigny Château became more of a house for living in than a fortress, with new Renaissance pavilions added. One was called Pavillon Sévigné, after Madame de Sévigné the brilliant letter-writing chronicler of Louis XIV's court, who stayed there for a few days and described it in a letter comparing it with her daughter's château at Grignan.

The pavilion is still there, a very elegant two-storey building. You can still see, too, the guard room gateway, prisons, vaults, impressive medieval walls, a huge fine Renaissance kitchen and Grande Salle where the lords dispensed justice. There are fine views from the terraces. Within the walls is the Collegiate church St Martin (thirteenth to fifteenth centuries).

In the setting of the seventeenth-century Abbaye du Gard, lay brothers have set up a hostel with twenty-eight rooms with running water, shared showers and conference room. The abbey is being restored. At Chaussée Trancourt over the river is a park called Samara showing the way of life in prehistoric times (tel. 22.95.09.10). Archaeological excavations are still taking place. There is canoeing on the Somme.

PIERREFONDS
[Oise]

The huge feudal château of Pierrefonds on the edge of the lovely Compiègne Forest, beside the attractive little town of Pierrefonds, is a pleasant folly, reconstructed for Napoleon III by Viollet-le-Duc 140 years ago when Napoleon was making the town into a fashionable spa. Viollet-le-Duc was very heavily criticized at the time, which is strange, for few criticized him for rebuilding the walled city of Carcassonne (except the architect who called it 'the most magnificent fake in the world') and no one complained when he heavily restored Notre-Dame in Paris. Pierrefonds is deeply impressive and I have a sneaking feeling that it tells me more about life in a feudal castle than any of the ruins I have seen.

There was a château here in the eleventh century. A new one was built at the end of the fourteenth century and beginning of the fifteenth by the Royal architect for Louis d'Orléans who became Regent and ruler of France when his brother Charles VI lost his reason. Louis was assassinated in 1407. Pierrefonds belonged to the poet-prince Charles d'Orléans (1391–1465), who was captured by the English at Agincourt and spent a happy twenty-five years in England composing roundels, ballads and poems in French and English. The Catholic League occupied it in the Wars of Religion of the sixteenth century. When Henri IV took it from them, he gave it to Antoine d'Estrées, father of the delightful Gabrielle d'Estrées, Henri's most beloved mistress. It was left to the son of her and Henri, Antoine, Duc de Vendôme, but he rebelled against Louis XIII's banning of Protestantism after Henri's death, so the château was confiscated and knocked down. In 1813 Napoleon I bought the ruins for a song. Napoleon III inherited the château and the Bonaparte family's *folie de grandeur*. He ordered the controversial reconstruction. The heroic names which he gave to the towers – Hector, Charlemagne, Arthur, Caesar and Godefroy, and the statues of Charlemagne, Alexander the Great, King Arthur, Caesar and Guillaume le Grand (William the Conqueror) are incongruous. The statue of Louis d'Orléans in the Court of Honour looks strange, too. Heroines from romances are shown over the monumental fireplaces in Napoleon's large apartments, one with the face of his Empress Eugénie, the others the faces of the young women of their court.

On the elegant façade of the chapel, the statue of St James has a face suspiciously like that of Viollet-le-Duc. (Château shut on Tuesday, Wednesday in winter.)

The town of Pierrefonds is situated beside an attractive little lake.

HOTEL

Étrangers, 10 rue Beaudon, Cuise-la-Motte (44.42.80.18). Pleasant view. ROOMS E–F. MEALS B–F.

RESTAURANT

Tour, 16 rue Beaudon (44.42.80.47). Beside the forest and lake. MEALS A–E. Shut Tuesday.

POIX-DE-PICARDIE
[Somme]

Deep in an attractive valley SW of Amiens, Poix is the centre of the Evoissons, with charming country roads among valleys where you meet no one but fishermen sitting beside the streams. Arrows direct you round a Circuit des Evoissons, through the villages of Guizancourt and Agnières (about 30km starting on the D920E).

Poix is 28km direct from Amiens by the N29 but a longer, much nicer way is to go south from Amiens by the little D8 beside the river Selle, then turn west at Conty on the D920 to Poix.

Poix was almost annihilated in June 1940, but has been successfully rebuilt.

TOURIST INFORMATION rue St Denis (high season – 22.90.08.25) and town hall (22.90.00.02)
MARKET Saturday morning (place République)

HOTELS
Cardinal, place République (22.90.08.23). Modern but pleasant, with outside terrace tables. ROOMS D. MEALS A–F.
Poste, 13 place République (22.90.00.33). Good cooking, simpler rooms. ROOMS C. MEALS A–E.

PONT-DE-BRIQUES
[Pas-de-Calais]

5km S of Boulogne, just before the D940 branches off the N1. The village is just off the N1 to the right coming from Boulogne, after St Léonard. Just before you cross the bridge in the village is a modest eighteenth-century château. There Napoleon stayed for the two years between 1803 and 1805 while he planned the invasion of England. His office was in the old walled town in Boulogne.

He took over a wing of the château. In the salon, he dictated the general plan of his future campaign against Austria, which led him to victory at Austerlitz. The château is being renovated. A small side-road, the D52, takes you in 2km to St Étienne-du-Mont from where a hill gives views to the dome of Boulogne Cathedral.

HOTEL

Hostellerie de la Rivière, 17 rue Gare (21.32.22.81). The reliable and pleasant cooking of Jean Martin has received a shot in the arm from the arrival of his son Dominique, who has imagination and a strong modern touch. You can still choose the finer classic Norman dishes of old – and personally I do! The restaurant now has a Michelin star, and is fashionable around Boulogne. Very nice, too. Rooms are much improved. ROOMS E. MEALS D–G. Shut 15 August–15 September; February holidays; Sunday evening, Monday.

LE PORTEL
[PAS-DE-CALAIS]

5km S of Boulogne, not far from the hoverport, Le Portel was the traditional beach for Boulogne families, especially in past times when Boulogne beach and casino were fashionable. It was a separate fishing village back in the fourteenth century, and looked like a fishing village when I first saw it in the late 1930s. Some very old fishermen's houses were built into the cliff caves. But it was ninety per cent destroyed by Allied bombing in the Second World War. The Germans had heavily fortified it, including modernizing the forts set up in the sixteenth century and Fort de l'Heurt built on an islet by Napoleon in 1804.

The sand beach is broken by rocks and a promenade stands over it.

Although it is away from the bathing beach, the hovercraft is somewhat unpopular with some locals because of its noise and disturbance. It has its own railway station (Boulogne-Aeroglisseurs) with fast trains to Amiens and Paris.

TOURIST INFORMATION place Poincaré (in season – 21.31.45.93)

MARKETS Tuesday, Friday
FESTIVAL February – big carnival and floats parade

HOTEL

Beau Rivage, place Mgr Bourgain, near beach (21.31.59.82).
Simple ROOMS B. MEALS A–C. Restaurant shut Friday, Saturday
and Sunday from 30 September–1 March.

RESTAURANT

Grand Large, rue Mar. Foch, near beach (21.31.71.51). Little
old-style restaurant where I have eaten superb fish for years.
Excellent value. MEALS A–E. Shut Friday evening 1 October–
1 May.

LE QUESNOY
[NORD]

A charming and remarkable little town SE of Valenciennes on
the D934. It has been fortified since the thirteenth century and
the remarkable thing is that its fortified walls are still intact and
the defensive system designed by Vauban looks very striking in
pink brickwork. Almost the whole town is still within these old
walls.

Charles V and Louis XIII had both had a hand in building
the battlements when Vauban started his work. Great trees,
whitewashed houses and much greenery have softened the
defences and there is a lovely walk round the battlements. Lakes
and moats still lap the walls on the NW and SE sides. The
waterways around the town are used for swimming, rowing and
sculling, canoeing and for fishing. Mormal Forest, with its lovely
walks and drives, is only 4km away.

By the west postern gate of the walls is a monument to the
New Zealand Rifle Brigade who, in 1918, took the strongly
defended town by scaling the walls under heavy enemy fire.

The town hall (1585) has a classical tower added in the
seventeenth century. Concerts are given by its carillon of bells.
Château de Potelle, a small medieval moated fortress built in
1290, is 2km E. You cannot go inside.

TOURIST INFORMATION rue Mar. Joffre (in season –
27.49.05.59)

HOTEL

Hostellerie du Parc, 7 rue Victor Hugo (Boulogne 27.49.02.42).
Six rooms. Good for regional dishes, including *flamiche au
maroilles*. Cheap, good value. ROOMS C. MEALS B–D. Restaurant
shut Sunday evenings, Monday.

RESTAURANT

Anzac, 2 rue Weibel (27.49.27.49). Another tribute to the New
Zealanders! MEALS B–F. Shut 15–30 September; February holidays; Sunday evening, Monday.

RAMBURES, CHÂTEAU DE
[SOMME]

A château with a remarkable history on an estate which has
belonged to the same family for 1000 years. Descendants of the
Rambures family, La Roche Fontenilles, still live there. The
medieval château stands 4km SW of Oisement on the little D180,
25km SE of Le Tréport and 25km S of Abbeville.

It was built in the fifteenth century during the Hundred
Years War and remained French though in territory held by the
English. It has four towers with pepper-pot roofs, all immensely
strong. It was built at a low level deliberately so that it had less
chance of being damaged by firing but the tower walls were
made high enough to prevent anyone scaling them. The walls
are between 3 and 7 metres thick and pierced by sixteen cannon
emplacements. The superb vaulted cellars housed the troops.
The drawbridge is still there. Outbuildings were added in the
seventeenth and eighteenth centuries and the chapel was built in
the nineteenth century.

In the English-style park and woods are very old and rare
trees. The Rambures family was first mentioned in 1058 but
came to prominence in the Hundred Years War.

David de Rambures, Grand-Master of the Crossbowmen of

France, was called 'Le Brave Rambures'. Henri IV stayed with him at the château on his way back from his great victory at Arques in 1589. They became close friends, especially after David saved Henri's life at the Battle of Ivry (1590). In the next generation Charles Rambures wisely became friendly with Louis XIII, who stopped that notorious demolition-fanatic Cardinal Richelieu from knocking down his château.

Inside are objets d'art and Picardie furniture from the fifteenth to seventeenth centuries. Visits daily except Wednesday, 1 March to 1 November; Sunday and public holiday afternoons, 2 November to end February.

RARAY
[Oise]

In the Renaissance château of this Valois hamlet close to the A1 motorway NE of Senlis, Jean Cocteau's great film *Beauty and the Beast* (*La Belle et La Bête*) was made. Dating mostly from the beginning of the seventeenth century, the château is renowned for the typically Renaissance decoration, particularly of the entrance courtyard (la cour d'Honneur). The sculptures of people of the seventeenth century and carved hunting scenes are quite remarkable. So are the sculptures on the great gateway at the NW of the park, showing the allegory of the *Virgin and the Unicorn*. You can visit the splendid Italian garden and exterior of the château on Saturday and Sunday afternoons from mid-March to mid-November. There is a Renaissance manor in the village.

RIVIÈRE
[Pas-de-Calais]

One of a group of pleasant villages 10km SW of Arras, little known although only 2 or 3km off the N25 at Beaumetz-lès-Loges. They include Grosville, Bretencourt and Bellacourt.

Rivière has a very beautiful church, St Vaast, built in 1767. Nearby is Château de Grosville, a charming, low manor house in brick and stone built in 1754 – almost a huge, elegant bungalow with dormer windows in its roof.

Bretencourt is a lovely village hiding several interesting houses and old farms. Its château has a fourteenth-century tower, the main house of 1775 and a nineteenth-century wing with a fine dovecot.

ROUBAIX
(NORD]

Manufacturing centre with more than 100,000 inhabitants which has become virtually part of Lille (*see* Major Towns, page 59). In the nineteenth century it was a big textile town. Now it concentrates mainly on wool, making clothes, household curtains, carpets and covers, and stockings. It is one of the biggest woollen goods producers in the EC. It is also the centre for big mail order companies.

Just south of Roubaix, in the village of Hem, is a beautiful modern chapel – Chapelle de Ste Thérèse-de-l'Enfant-Jésus et de la Sainte-Face, finished in 1958. A simple outline stands above the little white houses, with fine glass walls of truly warm and vibrant colour designs by the artist Manessier. The sculptures of the altar, crucifix and statue of St Thérèse are by the sculptor Dodeigne, and the imposing tapestry of la Sainte-Face is by Georges Rouault, one of the greatest modern artists of tapestries, stained glass and book illustrations. He died the year the church was opened.

TOURIST INFORMATION Town hall (Roubaix),
17 Grand'Place (20.70.70.02)
MARKETS Monday, Tuesday, Wednesday mornings;
Thursday, Saturday, Sunday

HOTEL

Flandres, 59 rue Holden, at Croix (20.72.35.01). ROOMS C–E. MEALS B–C. Restaurant shut 15 July–15 August; Saturday, Sunday.

RESTAURANT

Caribou, 8 rue Mimerel (20.70.87.08). Very good cooking, exceptional wine-cellar. Businessmen's favourite. MEALS F–G. Shut 15 July–31 August; Monday, Saturday lunch, and evenings except Friday, Saturday.

RUE
[SOMME]

Quiet little town bypassed by the D940 and D32 on the edge of the Marquenterre marshes and dunes, N of Le Crotoy, it is known mostly for hunting and fishing, which are two French religions. In summer we used to drive this way from Montreuil to Dieppe or into other parts of Seine Maritime just to avoid Abbeville's traffic!

Rue was a port in the Middle Ages but there are 8km of sand dunes now between the town and the sea. Left from its more important days is a really marvellous Flamboyant-Gothic chapel which has carved stone like delicate lace and a unique vaulted roof with starry pendants. Chapelle du St Esprit (the Holy Ghost) was for centuries a place of pilgrimage because of its crucifix. This is said to have been one of three miraculous crucifixes found by crusaders in Jerusalem, near to Golgotha. The other two went to a place in Italy and to Dives in Normandy. The people of Abbeville tried very hard to get their hands on Rue's holy relic, but Rue held on to it. Pilgrims brought prosperity in those days, as tourists do today. The chapel of the old pilgrims' hospice is still there – sixteenth century with wooden vaulting and statues from the fifteenth and sixteenth centuries.

HOTEL

Lion d'Or, 5 rue Barrière (22.25.74.18). Comfortable Logis with pleasant meals in an area short of hotels, if not fish restaurants. ROOMS D–E. MEALS A–D. Shut 15–20 October; December; Sunday evening from 1 January–31 March. Restaurant shut Sunday except July, August.

ST AMAND-LES-EAUX
[NORD]

The only spa in the Nord department, it is an historic town on the edge of the St Amand-Raismes Forest, now a Regional Nature Reserve. St Amand is only 10km NW of Valenciennes and 6km from the A23 motorway which, incredibly, runs through the nature reserve.

The spa is 4km E of the town by the D151 at Fontaine-Bouillon. The source was known to the Romans, who rarely missed a curative spring. When it was decided to exploit the springs in the seventeenth century, under the direction of Vauban, the military architect, wooden statues were found in the pool, left centuries before as *ex-voto* offerings by people hoping for a cure. The waters emerge at 26°C and are among the most radioactive in France. They are used to treat rheumatism and to help various injured parts of the body function again. The establishment was rebuilt after the Second World War and, like almost every spa, has a gambling casino. It is strange that people seeking health have for centuries sought also to destroy their wealth. Louis Bonaparte, who took the cure there in 1805, had the Drève du Prince (the Prince's Drive) made.

In 1793 Château de Fontaine-Bouillon, now disappeared, was the quarters of General Dumouriez, who had joined the Revolution as a liberal Girondist and led the Revolutionary armies successfully, defeating the Prussians at Valmy and the Austrians at Jernappes. He set out to capture the Netherlands but was comprehensively beaten at Neerwinden by the Austrians and fled to Fontaine-Bouillon, where he heard that he had been denounced in Paris as a traitor. So he became one – going over to the Austrians with Général Égalité, the ex-Duke of Chartres. His father was Philippe Égalité, ex-Duke of Orléans, who was now a member of the Revolutionary Government. Dumouriez wandered Europe, lived in England and died at Henley-on-Thames. Général Égalité lived in Twickenham but went back to France as Regent, and grabbed the crown as King Louis-Philippe. His father was arrested when his son joined the Austrians and was guillotined.

St Amand-les-Eaux's other claim to fame is the ruins of a Benedictine abbey. The charming belltower contains a museum. In it are some excellent local *faiences*, a section devoted to bells, and paintings by Louis Watteau of Lille, nephew of the great Watteau. The tower is 82 metres high, flanked by two turrets, and has a carillon of forty-seven bells, cast in Annecy in 1950. Concerts are given daily at noon and Saturday and Sunday evenings in summer.

St Amand-Raismes Forest has small roads going through it as well as the motorway, and many walking and horse-riding paths, a lake with a boating centre and several large ponds. The wild animals include boar, many deer of various types and wild goats.

TOURIST INFORMATION Beffroi (27.48.57.56)
MARKET Wednesday

RESTAURANT

Auberge de la Forêt, 92 rue Valenciennes (27.25.51.98). In the forest, so specializes in game. MEALS D–G. Shut Monday, Sunday evening.

St Gobain Forest

ST GOBAIN
[AISNE]

Centre of the renowned St Gobain glass, founded in 1692 in an
old château by order of Louis XIV's Chief Minister Colbert, who
was trying to stop France spending money on imports and to pay
off Louis' vast debts. It is on the edge of the vast St Gobain
Forest on a high plateau west of Laon – a beautiful forest of oak,
beech, ash, silver birch and poplars, rich in deer, with beautiful
forest roads, and marked pathways around hills and valleys. St
Gobain was an Irish monk-missionary; he is buried in the
churchyard.

HOTEL

Roses de Picardie, 11 rue Clemenceau, St Gobain (23.52.88.74).
Very friendly. Simple, clean bedrooms; no restaurant. ROOMS
A–C.

ST LEU-D'ESSERENT
[OISE]

Small town on the Oise river 6km NW of Chartres which has a
magnificent church standing high above the river, its apse on the
edge of the cliff. It is built of the stone of Avesnes, used later for
many cathedrals and for the palace of Versailles.

It looks particularly beautiful from the river-bridge. Most of
it dates from the twelfth century and is in pure early-Gothic
style. Apart from its two towers, the church has the distinct look
of a Greek temple. The modern stained glass by the master, Max
Ingrand, in no way clashes with the old. During restoration after
1944, remains of an earlier chapel were found. Of the Benedictine priory to which the church belonged, a fortified gate, two
walks of the twelfth-century cloister and a very old underground
room remain.

ST MICHEL FOREST
[*See* Hirson, page 152]

ST OMER
[Pas-de-Calais]

The more I get to know St Omer, the more I like it. It is a really pleasant town – a lovely place for a weekend. No wonder that its 300-year-old merchants' houses, its ancient shops and cafés in Grande'Place, tilting all ways, and its mysterious waterways still lure artists.

Built on rising ground above drained fertile marshlands packed with market gardens, only 39km from Dunkerque, 40km from Calais, and 53km from Boulogne, St Omer keeps its seventeenth- and eighteenth-century elegance, and its air of tranquillity.

The centre for me is the cobbled Grand'Place (place Maréchal Foch), not only because the dignified town hall with the tourist office is there, and that I can often park, but because it is *the* place to sit outside one of those ancient cafés and watch St Omer coming and going. The rivers Aa and Neuffossé and the canal, which joins a network of waterways to Dunkerque, Gravelines and Calais, made it a very busy port when ships were smaller. Seagoing vessels docked at the quays. Prosperous merchants built their fine mansions along wide streets. The low Flemish houses along the quays of the Aa were the houses of the working people.

The big public gardens made from the remains of Vauban's ramparts at the west side are a delight at any time of the year, but especially in autumn when the leaves are turning. They must be a real joy to the people of St Omer. (I could never get used to calling them 'les Audomarais' as the French do.) In the gardens is a heated swimming-pool, open from early June to end September.

Overlooking the gardens is the great basilica of Notre-Dame, formidable and majestic – a huge church from the twelfth century, with an enormous nave, and a strong tower from the fifteenth century decorated with arches. The nave is almost a museum, with so many sculpted tombs and statues, including the striking and realistic tomb of St Omer and the beautiful carved group *Grand Dieu de Thérouanne* from the thirteenth century. The polychrome marble screens to the chapel are superb, the 1558 astronomical clock bewilderingly complicated.

St Omer is still so rich in old buildings that you discover new ones on each visit. Oddly, the ruins of the Tour St Bertin, an old church tower, are possibly the most impressive.

The really elegant classical mansion of 1766, with a double-cross of Lorraine on the roof, is now the Sandelin museum (14 rue Carnot). Its ceramics collection, which includes a lot of old Delft ware, is wonderful. So is the gold and enamel pedestal of the Cross of St Bertin from the twelfth century. Tapestries are

Canal-side houses, St Omer

interesting. Paintings include good fifteenth- to seventeenth-century Flemish and Dutch works, including Brueghel, and a few very good French eighteenth- to nineteenth-century paintings shown alongside furniture of the period. I was fascinated by the scenes from bourgeois family life by Louis-Léopold Boilly (1761–1845), known mostly as a portrait painter. The *Jealous Old Man* is brilliant. The local nineteenth-century artist Alphonse Deneuville, who painted a lot of military scenes, is well represented.

The collection of clay pipes is fascinating. Pipe-making was an important local industry from the seventeenth to nineteenth centuries (museum shut Monday, Tuesday).

It is well worth visiting the Musée Henri-Dupuis in an eighteenth-century mansion (rue Henri-Dupuis) for its wonderful tiled old Flemish kitchen. Otherwise it is mostly a natural history museum, with many stuffed birds from the Arctic to Indonesia shown in mock-ups of their natural surroundings, and a collection of shells from all over the world (museum shut Monday, Tuesday).

St Omer is surrounded by fine wide boulevards, but beyond them big concrete apartment blocks have been built, blocking the fine old view of the town as you approach. At least they were not built in the middle of the town.

The Watergangs – the drainage canals which criss-cross the fertile former marshes to the N and E, are 300km long, bordered in the E by the Clairmarais Forest. Rich in pike, perch, bream, sandres and eels, these waterways are a joy to fishermen as well as to canoeists. They are still used to move produce in flat-bottomed motor boats from the market gardens alongside although now it is all packed neatly in boxes. I remember when they piled the produce in the punts and poled them along. The gardens grow superb vegetables, especially cauliflower, and more of them are growing flowers and fruit these days. At weekends in season the road to Clairmarais is lined with stalls selling the produce. St Omer people drive out there to buy.

You can take boat trips on the little canals and the big canals and rivers. For local trips, boats leave from Taverne Flamande (tel. 21.98.80.21) in St Omer or Moulin Rouge (tel. 21.38.35.14) in Clairmarais. Traditional barques go from 6 route de Clair-

marais (tel. 21.38.11.65). The boat *Emeraude* has three routes –
one round the Marais canals, another to Arques to see a unique
hydraulic boat-lift, left from 1887, and a third along the Aa to
Houlle (5km NW) for lunch. It leaves from the D209 Clairmarais road near the bridge of the Neuffossé canal
(21.98.66.74).

TOURIST INFORMATION boul. P. Guillain (21.98.08.51)
MARKETS Wednesday, Saturday

HOTELS

Bretagne, 2 place Vainquai (21.38.25.78). Well run by same
Beauvalet family as Georges V, Calais. Modern. Good cooking.
ROOMS D–F. MEALS F–G. GRILL A–C. Restaurant shut 2–15
January; Sunday evening, Saturday. Grill shut Saturday lunch,
Monday.

St Louis, 25 rue Arras (21.38.35.21). Simple, modernized rooms.
Evening restaurant. ROOMS B–E. MEALS A–F. Restaurant shut
lunchtime and Sunday.

Château Tilques, at Tilques, 6km NW by N42, N43, then lane to
right (21.93.28.99). The old 'Vert Mesnil' in nineteenth-century
château which became a priests' seminary. New luxury rooms.
Pleasant restaurant in converted stables. Recently bought by
Britons. In pleasant park. ROOMS F–G. MEALS E–G. Shut 24
December–2 January; Saturday lunch.

Hostellerie St Hubert, at Hallines, 6km by D928, D211
(21.39.77.77). Very recently converted from small manor in Aa
river valley. Only five rooms. Good cooking by young chef.
ROOMS E–F. MEALS C–G.

RESTAURANTS

Truye qui File, 8 rue Bleuets (21.38.41.34). Old local favourite,
very pleasant, welcoming. Good-value menus. MEALS C–F. Shut
August; Sunday evening, Monday.

Cygne, 8 rue Caventou (21.98.20.52). Bourgeoise house opposite
an eighteenth-century swan fountain. Popular locally. Good
value. Classic cooking. Twelve ways of preparing duck breast
(*magret*)! MEALS B–E. Shut 10–31 December; Saturday lunch,
Tuesday.

ST QUENTIN
[*See* Major Towns, page 64]

ST RIQUIER
[SOMME]

Called Centrule until AD645 when the hermit Riquier, a noble-man who set out to convert Le Ponthieu to Christianity, went to live in Crécy Forest and was buried in Centrule. A Benedictine monastery was set up there and became so prosperous that in 790 the Emperor Charlemagne handed it over to his son-in-law, the poet Angilbert, who has been compared with Homer. He reconstructed it using beautiful materials including marble

St Riquier

brought from Italy – quite a feat in those days. The abbey had three churches and was a great centre of pilgrimage, joined by a great cloister.

St Riquier is now on the D925 NE of Abbeville. Its abbey was restored in the seventeenth century. Now it is a cultural centre with a permanent display on Rural Life in Picardie, and other, temporary, exhibitions.

The great abbey-church was reconstructed several times. The present church has some thirteenth-century elements but is mostly fifteenth to sixteenth century in Flamboyant-Gothic. The square Flamboyant tower, which acts as a façade, is entirely sculpted – lavishly carved and full of statues. The interior is simple and beautiful. It contains a wooden Christ by François Girardon (1628–1715), leading sculptor of Louis XIV's reign and very classical. In the sixteenth-century treasury, devoted to the life of the Virgin, are fine wall paintings including one of Louis XIV by Jean Jouvenet (1644–1715) and an *Apparition of the Virgin to Ste Philomène* by Ducornet, a remarkable nineteenth-century artist who painted with his feet because he had no arms.

ST VALERY-SUR-SOMME
[SOMME]

A charming little port at the mouth of the Somme opposite Le Crotoy with a fine old fortified town above it which has two ancient gateways and ramparts around cobbled streets. The old houses are decked with flowers in summer. From up there you can see the port below, the estuary of sandbanks partly covered with vegetation, and the bay. You can see the sheep, too, cropping the greenery until the tide comes in.

Past the remains of an old abbey to the W, down in a dip, and sheltered by very old trees, is the old Mariners' Chapel with St Valery's tomb. Of the abbey, only the eighteenth-century abbot's château remains.

Into the port below William the Conqueror sailed from Dives in 1066 to pick up part of his army on his way to invading England. It is still a fishing port, although most of the boats land shellfish, and the *sauterelliers*, the shrimping boats, come in on the tide. In the First World War it was an important supply port for the British Army.

The little harbour attracts pleasure yachts, too, and a long promenade continues W. St Valery is becoming more popular as a small holiday resort, which is not surprising, for it has great charm and a lot of sand.

TOURIST INFORMATION On promenade in season
(22.60.93.50)
MARKET Sunday

HOTELS

Relais Guillaume de Normandie, quai Romerol (22.60.82.36). By the sea. Local and Norman dishes (*poulet en camembert*). ROOMS A–C. MEALS A–E. Shut 15 November–5 February except New Year's Eve; Tuesday.

Pilotes, 16 rue Ferté (22.60.80.39). Beside quai. Good fish *marmite*. ROOMS A–E. MEALS A–F. Shut 1 December–end February.

Port et des Bains, quai Blavet (22.60.80.09). Basic rooms. Wonderful-value fish meals. ROOMS A–B. MEALS A–D. Shut late part November.

SAMER
[PAS-DE-CALAIS]

Samer still has a genuine strawberry fair – on the Sunday nearest to 20 June. At other times it is an agricultural market for the villages and hamlets of the nearby Course valley. Although it is on the N1, it looks towards the countryside and villages eastward for its life. It has some small industries, like producing specialist parts for aircraft, but its major industry is still growing strawberries and making goats' milk cheese.

Samer Fair, on 14 September, was first held in the twelfth century.

MARKET Monday
FESTIVAL See above

SANGATTE
[PAS-DE-CALAIS]

History was made at the end of the long beach here on 25 July 1909, when Louis Blériot took off in his Blériot monoplane to be the first man to cross the Channel in a heavier-than-air craft. It will be made again near Sangatte when the Eurotunnel to England opens. Then, perhaps, the cleaning up can begin. Tunnelling does not improve the countryside. But at least the archaeologists are happy. They have made most interesting finds, many now in Calais museum. You can visit a tunnel museum on the site, showing the whole plan.

After his sea invasion of England plans collapsed, Napoleon considered tunnelling from here, but soon gave up the idea. A tunnel was started in 1877 but was killed by an outcry in Britain. Led by the great army hero, Viscount Wolseley, the military men painted horrific pictures of a foreign power pouring an army through the tunnel and taking over England, presumably while every Englishman slept. No doubt they had been shaken by the quick invasion of France by the Prussians in 1870.

On the cliff is a monument to the men of the Dover Patrol – a legend in their day but now almost forgotten. They manned minesweepers – many converted from trawlers – which in all weathers and in all conditions swept the Channel for mines and kept it open for British shipping in the First World War. A book about them, simply called *Dover Patrol*, was written by W. W. Jacobs, the very funny writer about barges and sailors, who died in 1943. But who remembers him now, except perhaps for his gruesome short story called 'The Monkey's Paw'?

SARS-POTERIES
[NORD]

Sars-Poteries is 9km NE of Avesnes by the N2 and the attractive D962, another of those interesting places S of Maubeuge and east of Avesnes-sur-Helpe which few travellers know. Starting with pottery, the people switched to glass-making in the nineteenth century and it became a world centre for making glass tableware and drinking glasses until the 1930s depression. The industry closed in 1938, but recently has started again and its workshop teaches young people the art of glass-blowing. There is a fascinating glass museum (open afternoons Saturday and Sunday; daily during school summer holidays).

RESTAURANT

Auberge Fleurie, 67 rue Gén-de-Gaulle (27.61.62.48). Very good young chef draws people from far around. Alan Lequy deserves his Michelin star. MEALS E–G. Shut end January–20 February; 15–31 August; Sunday evening, Monday.

SEBOURG
[NORD]

Country retreat for the people of Valenciennes (*see* page 209), which is 11km W. It is at the end of the green valley of the Autell river, and the Grande Randonnée 122 (long distance footpath) passes through it. The Belgian border is less than 2km away.

HOTEL

Jardin Fleuri, on D250 (27.26.53.44). Rooms at the bottom of the garden, rather simple. Excellent-value meals. ROOMS B–C. MEALS C–D. Restaurant shut Sunday evenings.

SECLIN
[NORD]

Industrial town on the D925 S of Lille, of which it is virtually a suburb.

The ancient hospital, SW of the town, was founded in the thirteenth century by Marguerite de Flandres, and is still in use. The present seventeenth-century buildings in Flemish Baroque are built in stone and brick and well sculpted. The arcaded courtyard is beautiful.

The thirteenth-century parish church of St Piat has a carillon of forty-two bells in its tower, installed in 1933. Concerts are
given at 11 a.m. on Mondays and on holidays.

Forgeron, 17 rue Roger Bouvry (20.90.09.52). 'Three-chimney'
Logis. Roger Belot, expert of Flanders classical cookery, has
given in to a few modern dishes as well. Very good cooking.
ROOMS C–F. MEALS C–G. Shut August; Saturday evening,
Sunday.

SENLIS
[OISE]

Don't be fooled – behind the traffic-ridden commercial town
which lines the N17 Paris road lies one of the most charming old
towns in the north. Only 50km from Paris and with the A1
motorway running alongside it, Senlis is almost surrounded by
beautiful forests – Halatte, Chantilly and Ermenonville, which
stretch for miles north and south. It is only 11km E of Chantilly.
This area of France, from Chantilly to Laon, is very beautiful.

When Louis V, last of the Carolingian kings, was killed in a
hunting accident in 987, the nobles met in the Château de Senlis
and elected Hugues Capet King of the Franks. His Kingdom of
France was little bigger then than the Île de France of today.
The future kings of France were his descendants, but gradually
they forsook the Château de Senlis for the greater delights of
Compiègne and Fontainebleau, though until Henri IV they
dropped in occasionally.

Some of the château still stands, including a square keep,
and the eighteenth-century priory in the grounds, now containing a hunting museum. In the park of the château is a
gorgeous statue of Diana the Huntress with her arm round a
handsome stag. (Château and museum both shut Tuesday and
Wednesday morning.)

The splendid cathedral of Notre-Dame, overlooking pleasant place Parvie, was begun in 1153, ten years before Notre-

Dame in Paris. Its belfry still dominates the town, the spire reaching to 80 metres. The west Romanesque façade has a main doorway carved with the representation of death, resurrection and the coronation of the Virgin, a doorway copied for the cathedrals of Chartres, Notre-Dame in Paris, Amiens and Reims. The high interior has a great gallery which runs above the side-aisles on both sides of the nave and choir.

Just to the east side of the quiet little place Parvie is the former Bishop's palace, thirteenth century but altered in the seventeenth century. It is now a museum of art and archaeology. Just east of that is the eleventh- to sixteenth-century church of St Pierre, converted long ago into a covered market. The church of St Framberg near the Bishop's Palace is twelfth century and is now a music centre called Franz Liszt auditorium, converted by the pianist Giorgy Cziffra.

One of the greatest joys in Senlis is to explore the fascinating narrow streets and cobbled alleys with fine old houses clustered on the south hill from the cathedral, down steep slopes to the river Nonette. The old ramparts have become boulevards lined with trees and tubs bright with flowers.

TOURIST INFORMATION place Parvis (44.53.06.40)
MARKETS Tuesday and Friday mornings
FESTIVALS March – Festival d'Art Baroque; last
weekend September – Fête Rendez-vous de Septembre;
September – Salon of Ancient Arms

HOTELS

Hostellerie Porte Bellon, 51 rue Bellon (44.53.03.05). Very popular and heavily booked. Logis de France on boulevard. ROOMS B–E. MEALS C–G. Shut 20 December–10 January. Restaurant shut Friday.

Nord, 110 rue République (44.53.01.16). Simple Logis on the busy main through-road. Rooms A–D. MEALS C. Restaurant shut Wednesday mid-winter.

RESTAURANTS

Formanoir, 17 rue Châtel (44.53.04.39). Sixteenth-century former convent in the old town in steep cobbled street with good old-style cooking. Choice of restaurant (pricey) or cheaper bistro (shut Sunday). MEALS C–E.

Vert Galant, 15 place Henri IV (44.53.60.15). In the heart of the old town in an old house, the dining-room is down in a medieval cellar. Warm, cosy, not enough tables, so book. In summer there are more tables in the garden. Good-value cheaper menus. MEALS C–F. Shut 10–25 August; February school holidays; Sunday evening, Monday.

SOISSONS
[AISNE]

Deeply involved in early French history from AD486 when Clovis the Frank defeated the Romans here. His son, Clotaire I, made it his capital. It remained a capital until 923 when Charles the Simple was defeated in battle under its walls.

Alas, it suffered terribly in three wars – the Franco-Prussian War of 1870–71, the First World War and the Second World War, and is virtually a new town, although some excellent buildings have survived.

Soissons is important now as an agricultural centre. The river Aisne runs alongside and it is the hub of roads to Compiègne, St Quentin, Laon, Reims, Château-Thierry and the N2 to Paris.

The huge Gothic cathedral, begun in the twelfth century but a wreck by 1918, has been sympathetically restored. It is graceful, simple and dignified. The north transept is delightful, with glowing thirteenth- to fourteenth-century windows and Rubens' glorious picture *Adoration of the Shepherds*, which he painted as a gift to the Franciscans who nursed him through a nasty illness. Of the original abbey founded in 1076, where Thomas à Becket lived for nine years, all that survives are the impressive façade, a refectory and cellar and parts of the fine cloisters. That was Napoleon's fault. In 1805 he issued an Imperial decree, to which the Bishop of Soissons agreed, ordering that the beautiful abbey should be pulled down and the materials used to repair the cathedral. Only because of a great public outcry was the façade saved.

The remains of the Abbey of St Léger, wrecked in 1567 by

Protestants, house the museum. It contains some interesting paintings, especially two by the eighteenth-century Venetian Pellegrini and landscapes by Boudin (1824–98), the great master of landscape painting, and Gustave Courbet (1819–77), a socialist who preached realism in painting against idealization and covered a wide field from sensuous nudes to landscapes and still life. (Museum shut Tuesday.)

TOURIST INFORMATION 1 ave Gén-Leclerc
(23.53.08.27)
MARKETS Wednesday, Saturday

HOTELS

Lion Rouge, 1 rue Alliaume (23.53.31.52). Best all-round hotel; in town centre. ROOMS B–E. MEALS B–G. Restaurant shut Saturday evening, Sunday.

Picardie, 6 rue Neuve St-Martin (23.53.21.93). Comfortable, dull, cheap. Interesting regional dishes. ROOMS C–D. MEALS B–D. Restaurant shut Sunday evening.

STEENVOORDE
[NORD]

True little Flemish town 8km SE of Cassel on the D948. Its houses with red roofs are painted in Flemish style. It has a renowned giant named Yan den Houtkapper – a wood-cutter who made Charlemagne a pair of shoes which never wore out. Wooden clogs, I should think. He is, of course, carried at fêtes and festivals. Steenvoorde once made woollen cloth. Now it has one of the best-known dairies in the north.

FESTIVAL October – Fête de Houblon (Hops)

STELLA PLAGE
[Pas-de-Calais]

Family beach resort which almost runs into Le Touquet. Sands, dunes and forest, with seasonal shops and many summer bungalows and villas. 3km inland is the old village of Cucq on D940. Cucq was a port in the twelfth century, but is now cut off from the sea by dunes. There are several small seasonal hotels in Stella Plage, which are excellent for children.

Tourist Information Boul. Labrasse (seasonal – 21.94.75.22)

HOTEL
Sables d'Or, 1184 ave Concorde (21.94.75.22). Very simple rooms. Very good value meals. Rooms B–C. Meals B–E. Open 1 May–15 September.

THÉROUANNE
[Pas-de-Calais]

Village in the Lys valley 15km S of St Omer which, until the sixteenth century, was a very important fortified ecclesiastical city, with a twelfth-century cathedral which was one of the most beautiful in northern France, and two abbeys. Its bishops were rich and powerful. One became the notorious Avignon Pope, Clément VII. In 1553 the Emperor Charles V captured the city and had it razed literally to the ground. All that remains of the cathedral is a sculpted group called the Grand Dieu de Thérouanne, now in St Omer Cathedral.

Excavations have gone on since 1961 and there is an archaeological museum (open Monday to Friday). Restoration has begun on an attractive chapel with a belltower.

Another church was built last century on the foundations of an earlier one. Its stained-glass windows show the arms of the Bishops from 630–1553.

Therouanne is now an agricultural village with fishing in the river Lys and a public lake.

LE TOUQUET
[Pas-de-Calais]

Walk round the boutiques, see the families unloading their cars of children's cycles, toys, dogs, cases of household equipment, books, even canaries in cages, on a Friday night, carry the lot into their apartments and almost immediately start to fill the shops, streets, cafés and restaurants and you know why Le Touquet is still called 'Paris-Plage'.

The name was invented by the owner of the Paris newspaper *Figaro*, M. Villemessant, in 1874, when he went to stay with Victor Daloz, a Paris lawyer, who had bought the whole coast from Point du Touquet to Merlimont (1606 hectares) in 1837 for 120,100F when the State was trying to unload it. It had been just dunes when he bought it, but he planted maritime pines with such success that a forest grew. *Figaro* plugged Le Touquet as the future bathing resort of Paris, to be 'more beautiful than Trouville', which was the fashionable resort in those days. A hotel was built and plots were offered for building villas. But in twenty years only 173 buildings had been put up and Daloz sold out to a London syndicate set up by a businessman called Stoneham. Le Touquet took off. They built tennis courts, a golf course, a swimming-pool on the sands, a race-track and riding school, hotels and a casino. Villas were built in the forest.

In the First World War it became a hospital town, with wounded soldiers in the hotels, but after that war it grew into a very fashionable international playground, with more lovely villas of the rich in the forest, less expensive villas for the bourgeoisie along the promenade and Grand Hotels such as the Westminster and the even grander Ermitage.

British millionaires and stage stars who included Noël Coward and his set and stage stars from Paris bought the very pricey villas in the delightful forest. The Bright Young Things, sons and daughters of the rich, disported themselves in the forest and the casino. The Plage was for lesser mortals. Private planes from Croydon, Lympne, Paris and Brussels filled the airfield.

Then came the Second World War. The Anglophile Mayor Dr Pouget was arrested by the Gestapo. Hitler's Todt Organiza-

tion moved in slave labour to make Le Touquet part of the
Nazis' West Wall against Allied Invasion.

Dr Pouget was back as Mayor in 1961. New British millionaires moved into the forest villas, including Sir Bernard Docker,
colourful boss of Daimler cars, who had a gold-plated car, his
ex-showgirl wife Nora and their flamboyant friends. Then came
jet travel. The British flew away to the Caribbean, leaving
behind only the names of their villas – Byways, Lone Pine,
Anchorage – among the pine and silver birch trees. The
Ermitage became a block of expensive flats. Many of the villas on
the promenade with their turrets and wooden balconies gave
way to small blocks of apartments. Parisian and Belgian indus-
trialists, stockbrokers and lawyers moved into the forest villas,
Parisian families into the apartments. The British are mere
visitors these days.

Even Flavio's Michelin-starred restaurant is no longer a
British ex-patriates' club, but has French gourmets eating its
excellent but extravagantly priced meals.

The Parisians have at last taken over and Le Touquet is as
pleasantly lively as ever, still with elegance in the forest, the
Westminster and the shops around it, the golf club and the
riding school. As well as discos, nightclubs and all sorts of restaurants, it has all kinds of international sports meetings, including golf, tennis, horse-racing and show-jumping, and
exhibitions and concerts through much of the year. The priciest
boutiques close for the winter but much remains open, especially
on weekends. And there is always Serge Pérard's superb fish
shop in rue Metz, where mountains of fresh oysters, mussels,
prawns and clams, plaice, cod, turbot and red mullet disappear
before your eyes as eager customers buy them. It is a take-away,
too, for fish pâtés and Serge's fish soup renowned all over
France, and a famous fish restaurant which, on Sunday lunchtime, develops into a Brueghel-like scene as French families
work their way through plate after plate of fish – and yards of
fresh baked bread with litres of Gros Plant and Muscadet wines,
while waiters literally run to keep them supplied. That to me is
the spirit of Le Touquet – not lounging on its enormous sands
or lazing in its dunes. I still love the place – even the mad scene
in season in Griffmode, which every woman under fifty knows is

Sand sailing, Le Touquet

the place for a clothes bargain: the noise makes an aviary sound like a snooker hall during a championship final, and, as my friend Roger Macdonald wrote, 'Changing rooms are such chaos that it is quite feasible to leave wearing someone else's underwear.'

TOURIST INFORMATION Town hall (21.05.17.55)
In season: Palais de l'Europe, place de l'Ermitage
(21.05.21.65)
MARKETS Thursday, Saturday; also Monday in summer
FESTIVALS Many – ask at Tourist Office

HOTELS

Westminster, ave Verger (21.05.48.48). Almost back to its grandest days. All comforts, service and huge rooms with prices starting around 650F for a double (1991). MEALS Restaurant (dinner only) E–G. Coffee shop A–E. Open I March–1 December.
Manoir, at Golf Club 2½km from Le Touquet (21.05.20.22). 'Old country house' style, complete with armour. Very comfort-

able. Swimming-pool. Rooms very expensive (from 650F in 1991). MEALS F–G.

Plage, boul. Dr Pouget (21.05.03.22). On promenade. No restaurant. ROOMS C–E.

RESTAURANTS

Flavio-Club Forêt, 1 ave Verger (21.05.10.22). See text. Magnificent fish. Very elegant. Carte too expensive. MEALS G. Shut 1 January–28 February; Wednesday.

Café des Arts, 80 rue Paris (21.05.21.55). Good, imaginative but not chi-chi dishes in chi-chi art-deco surroundings. Young chef from Le Touquet's famous hotel school. MEALS D–G. Shut Monday, Tuesday except July, August.

Serge Pérard, 67 rue Metz (21.05.13.33). See text. MEALS C–G.

Charlotte, 35 rue St Jean (21.05.32.11). Bistro popular with young people. Gets crowded but very good value. Take-away shop. MEALS B–E. Shut Wednesday low season.

TOURCOING
[NORD]

Merged now with Lille in one huge industrial area. (*See* Major Towns, page 59.)

MARKETS Daily except Sunday

TRIE-CHÂTEAU
[OISE]

Village 4km E of Gijor on right bank of the river Troesne. In the château, built in the eleventh century but considerably altered in the seventeenth century, the Prince of Conti invited Jean-Jacques Rousseau to stay in 1767. There the political philosopher finished his great autobiography *Confessions*, which he had begun in England at Wootton Hall when a guest of the Scottish philosopher David Hume. For a man whose writings are claimed by some to have contributed to the French Revolution, Rousseau was much liked by the nobility and seemed to have a liking for their hospitality in their beautiful châteaux. He died when a guest of the Marquis de Mirabeau. Rousseau's greatest work, which became the bible of the Revolution, was called *The Social Contract* (*Contrat Social*) and began, 'Man is born free and everywhere is in chains', and launched the slogan 'Liberty, Equality, Fraternity'.

A round tower and the lower parts of two more are all that remain of the eleventh-century château.

VALENCIENNES
[NORD]

I have met French people from the south of France who did not know where Valenciennes was. So much for French interest in one of its most important industrial cities, which refines petrol, makes cars, paint and railway equipment, to name but a few of its activities. It has the only major condom factory in France, set up by the British – ironic, considering the 'French letter' was truly a French invention.

Valenciennes was one of the blackest spots of French unemployment after the coal-mining industry collapsed, but the French government gave financial aid to new industries and excellent retraining to miners.

It did have a fine ancient city centre built in wood, until the Germans poured over the nearby Belgian border and bombarded it in 1940, and the Allies, chasing the Germans back again, knocked down much that had been missed before.

It is 32km NE of Cambrai where the A2 and A23 motorways meet. The St Amand-Wallens Forest begins only 3km NW with its pleasant walks and drives, and the lovely Mormal Forest is only 20km SE, with the charming Avesnois countryside a few kilometres the other side of it.

Valenciennes was for centuries an artistic centre, especially for sculptors and artists. Jean Froissart (1333–1405), the poet historian, was born there. He not only told us more about the

Middle Ages than any other man, but was also more entertaining and impartial. By the eighteenth century it had a school, academy and salon of fine arts.

Among the well-known sculptors and painters who came from Valenciennes were André Beauneuve (fourteenth century), the sculptor Antoine Pater (1670–1747) and his son the painter Jean-Baptiste Pater (1695–1736), pupil and imitator of Watteau. So did the great Antoine Watteau himself (1684–1721), the Rococo painter who invented *fêtes galantes* paintings in which elegant people wander in a dream world of music, conversation and amorous dalliance, and his nephew and great-nephew Louis and François Watteau.

Antoine Watteau was born at 39 rue de Paris and inevitably a square, place Watteau, is named after him, but it is sometimes called place Géry. It contains a statue of him by the local sculptor Jean-Baptiste Carpeaux (1827–75), who is credited with revitalizing French sculpture in the nineteenth century. His best work was the beautiful marble group of *The Dance* placed in the façade of l'Opéra in Paris in 1869. It was so vital and brazenly erotic that it was covered with ink by puritanical Parisians and is now in the Louvre.

Carpeaux has a whole room devoted to him in Valenciennes' Musée de Beaux Arts, on boulevard Watteau (shuts Tuesday). It includes finished bronzes and marbles and the maquettes of his major works, including *The Dance*, his Watteau monument and *Défence de Valenciennes*, which used to crown the town hall, was destroyed in the Second World War and replaced by a copy.

Watteau has two paintings – an early allegorical painting *True Happiness* and a fine portrait of the sculptor Antoine Pater.

There are two altar pieces by Rubens but the best work is Rubens' *Landscape with Rainbow*. The huge museum is rich in fifteenth- to seventeenth-century Flemish paintings.

2km NE at St Saulve, there is a very modern Carmelite convent (1966) in rue Barbusse which you can visit. It is built in geometric shapes of concrete designed by the sculptor Szekely.

Tourist Information 1 rue Askièvre (afternoons – 27.46.22.99)

HOTEL

Grand, 8 place Gare (27.46.32.01). Fine old grand hotel, modernized. Double glazed. ROOMS E–F. MEALS C–G.

RESTAURANT

Alberoi, Buffet Gare, 1 place Gare (27.46.86.30). Another station buffet which is the best restaurant in town. MEALS D–G. Shut Sunday evening.

VERVINS
[AISNE]

Capital of the old Thierache country SW of Hirson which rises as high as 250 metres and produces cider apples, milk, cream and butter for Paris and some Maroilles cheese. Pigs are fed on the skimmed milk.

Vervins has handsome streets of slate-roofed houses and remains of medieval ramparts. The thirteenth-century church with a sixteenth-century tower has sixteenth-century murals and a huge animated and colourful painting by Jouvenet (1699) of Christ eating in the house of Simon. In a big sixteenth-century house Château Coigny, now the *sous-préfecture*, Henri IV of France and Philippe II of Spain made a peace treaty in 1598 (*see* Hôtel Tour du Roy, below).

TOURIST INFORMATION 1 place Gén-de-Gaulle (in season – 23.98.09.92)

HOTEL

Tour du Roy, 45 rue Gén. Leclerc (23.98.00.11). Henri IV slept here in 1598 when it was a manor house and locals claim that it is where he was proclaimed King of France. An old, turreted house forms part of the old ramparts and town gate. In the seventeenth century it was a debtors' prison. The men were kept in a cellar below the kitchen, while the women were put in the tower where the jailer was allowed to sleep, to make sure that they were comfortable! The welcome at the inn is great, the regional cooking by Annie Desvignes has earned a Michelin star and the honeymoon suite up a circular staircase in the prison tower has a double bath. ROOMS D–G. MEALS D–G. Shut 15 January–15 February; Sunday evening, Monday lunch low season.

VILLENEUVE D'ASCQ
[NORD]

A new town 8km E of Lille by D941 with 60,000 people, built up since 1970 from three small communes. One of them, Annapes, had been made the site of the prestigious Science University of Lille in 1960–65. The new town has pedestrian pathways, totally avoiding traffic, various-style modern apartment blocks, a stadium holding 30,000 people and Espace Rose des Vents, an arena for concerts, exhibitions and theatre. There is a museum of modern art with a good collection of works from 1900–40, including many cubist paintings by masters (shut Monday, Tuesday and Wednesday morning).

The name Ascq was kept as a tribute to eighty-five people of that commune taken as hostages by the Germans in the Second World War and shot because the local people continued to fight in the Resistance.

VILLERS-COTTERÊTES
[AISNE]

The kings of France had a hunting lodge château here in the twelfth century, but the English destroyed it in 1429, so François I, the great collector of châteaux, had a vast Renaissance château built in 1532. Here in 1539 he made a decree that every birth in France must be registered in French and Latin in the parish register. Previously only noble births were registered.

Louis XIV had a garden laid out there by Le Nôtre, who designed the Versailles gardens.

Villers-Cotterêtes is a pleasant residential town on the edge of the attractive Retz Forest, 23km SW of Soissons on the N2.

Alexandre Dumas, the novelist, was born here in 1803 at a house which is now 46 rue Alexandre Dumas and has a museum of his manuscripts and first editions. His uniform of the Académie française is also on display here. It had never occurred to me that the Académicians had uniforms. His father, who was the son of a marquis and a coloured girl from the colony of Haiti, became a General in the French army but had to retire to his wife's home in Villers-Cotterêtes because he insisted on remaining a Republican when Napoleon I had become Emperor. Alexandre was four when his father died and when he was twenty and working for a lawyer his mother told him that she was down to her last 253 francs. He took 53F from her, played the local postmaster at billiards, betting the 53F against a ticket on the stage-coach for Paris, won, and set off for the capital. His beautiful handwriting got him a job in the secretariat of the Duc d'Orléans, who later became King Louis Philippe. Dumas first became known in 1829 for his play about Henri III. He wrote very many successful plays but it had always been his wish to write historical novels. He made fortunes from *The Three Musketeers*, *The Count of Monte Cristo* and others, but ran through the lot and left Paris finally for his son's house in Dieppe with only two gold napoleons to his name.

The château, which became the property of the Duc d'Orléans, is now an old people's home, but is open daily to the public. It has a superb Renaissance grand staircase. The old people sit in the courtyard surrounded by what were once the royal apartments. All that remains of Le Nôtre's great garden is a royal drive 3km into the forest.

7km W from Villers-Cotterêtes, just off the D32, is the village of Vez, the original capital of Valois. The remains of its once-important thirteenth-century château on a wooded hillside still look very grand.

Tourist Information Syndicat d'Initiative, 2 place A. Briand (23.96.30.03)

HOTELS

Régent, 26 rue Gén. Mangin (23.96.01.46). Old coaching inn which dates back to the sixteenth century, and became a stables. Restored in 1968. It has no restaurant. Rooms C–E.

Commerce, 17 rue Gén. Mangin (23.96.19.97). Seven simple rooms but good-value restaurant. ROOMS B–C. MEALS B–E. Shut 15–31 August; end January–14 February; Sunday evening, Monday.

VIMY RIDGE
[PAS-DE-CALAIS]

As you approach Arras from the NW you can see on the horizon two great white 'fingers' pointing into the sky. This is the huge Canadian war memorial at Vimy Ridge – a truly monumental tribute to the 74,000 Canadian soldiers who died in France in the First World War. You can reach it on a left turn off the N17 Lens road from Arras just before the village of Vimy 10km N of Arras. The A26 motorway now passes near it. During the Battle of Arras in 1917 four Canadian Divisions stormed the ridge, a German strongpoint. They took it – but the battle was a stalemate. It is a truly imposing and dignified monument. From its great plinth, like a solid wall of defence, you can see far across the old coal-mining area around Lens. Some trenches have been left from the battle and from 1 May to 30 September a guide will take you round them. The land around the memorial is Canadian territory.

LE WAST
[PAS-DE-CALAIS]

Very pleasant little village on the D127 just before it crosses the N42 from Boulogne (19km W). It has old houses round a green and a long manor house, Manoir de Huisbois, opposite two inns. Traffic has become a little heavier, otherwise it would be a pretty little hideaway. The manor has become a centre for country crafts and protection of the countryside. You can hire bikes here to explore the lanes.

The church, built before and altered after the crusades, has Arabic decorations on its doorway.

Outside Colembert, the hamlet to the E, is the great Château de Colembert, reached on D252 (3km), which you can also see from the N42. It stands at the foot of Mont Dauphin (201 metres high). It was reconstructed in the eighteenth century and has two wings and stone balustrades above the moat which surrounds it.

Le Wast's fête and horse fair in late September is popular in the whole area.

HOTEL

Hostellerie du Château des Tourelles (21.33.34.78). Forget the 'château' – this is a fin-de-siècle house. Good regional cooking, excellent fish from Boulogne. Smiling service. Earlier problems ironed out. Rooms in house far better than in extension. ROOMS C–D. MEALS C–F. Shut 14–22 February; Monday lunch.

RESTAURANT

Cornet d'Or (21.33.31.33): true old village inn with old-style country meals. MEALS A–C.

MONT WATTEN
[NORD]

A hill at the western end of the Flanders hills and the Audomarais marshes, dominating the Aa river valley and the plain of Flanders. Its position has been used to effect in wars by commanders – from the French commander Turenne in the Battle of the Dunes in 1658, to the German tank commander Guderian in 1940. It has a windmill, remains of an abbey, including a Gothic tower, and a good view over the river Aa, canals and the Eperlecques Forest. Guderian hid his tanks in the forest but to the great surprise of the Germans a French hydroplane came along each night and dropped a bomb of 1000kg – quite big in those days. It came from a base at Rochefort in Charente-Maritime. In June, the same plane dropped a bomb on Berlin.

WIMEREUX
[PAS-DE-CALAIS]

Wimereux, only 6½km from Boulogne and popular with British families as a seaside resort from the beginning of the century until the Second World War, still has some faded charm, despite damage in a storm quite recently, and the mysterious houses along the promenade which seem permanently boarded up. It has long stretches of hard sand and rock pools which delight children, and an old-fashioned main street which is nostalgic although too traffic-laden in summer.

In 1909 it was at the terminus of the 'new' electric tram from Boulogne, and soon it had villas, hotels and a casino. The promenade was built in 1920 and Wimereux prospered.

The great Monsieur Hamiot came from his corner brasserie in Boulogne and made the Atlantic Hotel famous, with its charcoal grill cooking absolutely fresh fish right alongside the beach. The Atlantic prospered, and its upstairs restaurant got a Michelin star; then it was all modernized, with a huge electric grill and spit at the end of the big dining-room, so that you could watch M. Hamiot cooking your chicken or Dover sole while you started with his superb crab pâté. There is a picture somewhere from a magazine of me helping him in the 1970s. He had two Michelin stars. Gourmets crossed the Channel just for a meal there. Others came from Paris and Brussels. Then his sons took over. The stars went; the Atlantic was sold.

I still cannot solve the mystery of Wimereux's decay and the closed houses. It still has so much potential, and pleasant restaurants with wonderful fish. There is also a golf course, sailing club and school, tennis and sea fishing.

TOURIST INFORMATION Town hall, rue Carnot
(21.32.46.29)
FESTIVALS May – Shellfish Fête; August – Mussels Fête

HOTELS

Centre, 78 rue Carnot (21.32.41.08). Delightful period piece. Run by same family for many years. Some new bedrooms. Excellent-value meals, loved by locals. ROOMS B–E. MEALS B–E.

Shut one week early June; 15 December–15 January. Restaurant shut Monday.

Atlantic, Digue de Mer (21.32.41.01). See text. Eleven comfortable rooms. Still serves very good fish. ROOMS E. MEALS D–G. Open 15 March–15 November.

Paul et Virginie, 19 rue Gén. de Gaulle (21.32.42.12). Long since converted from stables of mansion. Very friendly family. Nice atmosphere. Family cooking. ROOMS C–E. MEALS B–F. Shut 15 December–20 January. Restaurant shut Tuesday in winter; Sunday evening.

WISQUES
[PAS-DE-CALAIS]

In the vast château here, 6km SW of St Omer, with a fifteenth-century tower and much of the rest eighteenth century, a Benedictine abbey has been installed, called Abbaye St Paul. A little campanile close to the chapel houses a bell weighing 2600kg, cast in 1470 for St Bertin abbey in St Omer. The monks perform the Gregorian Chant each morning at 9.45 a.m. They make, show and sell ceramics and pottery.

On a hill along the D212 past the Petit Château (1770) is another Benedictine Abbey, Notre-Dame, in a charming nineteenth-century building. You can visit the chapel.

HOTEL

Sapinière (21.95.14.59). Simple inn, recovered from a bad patch; bedrooms improved. Flemish cooking, with good St Omer vegetables. ROOMS E MEALS B–E.

WISSANT
[PAS-DE-CALAIS]

A Welsh soldier named Davies married a French woman after the First World War, took over an old black-and-white inn called the Normandie in Wissant, and started a fashion, particularly among Fleet Street journalists, for taking their girlfriends or wives and families over for weekends and holidays. That started again after the Second World War, when the Davies family, who had sensibly fled to Wales, returned, and the son took over.

Wissant has huge sands and dunes, 12km long, a few local fishermen drying nets on the beach, modern villas in the dunes, a little chapel with a twelfth-century choir, baker's shop, café, chemist, a windmill with a little museum, three hotels and a campsite.

MARKET Wednesday

HOTELS

Vivier, place l'Église (21.35.93.61). Logis with excellent fish. ROOMS C–E. MEALS A–E. Shut 15 November–15 March.
Bellevue, rue Paul Crampel (21.35.91.07). Once the 'Grand Hotel' of Wissant. Comfortable Logis. ROOMS D–E. MEALS A–C. Shut 15 November–15 March.
Normandy (21.35.90.11). See text. Attractive inn, dining-room. Bedrooms modernized. Prices not known.

WORMHOUT
[NORD]

Hout means wood in Flemish and Wormhout is in the middle of the Flemish Houtland, spreading between the hills and the Blootland, which is Maritime Flanders with waterways.

It is a very typical little Flemish town on the D916 between Bergues and Cassel, W of the A25 motorway. It has a working windmill, La Briarde, from 1756, which still grinds away despite storms and a few technical problems. Guided tours of the mill are given from 1 May to 30 October except on Saturday and Sunday mornings; in the low season they are only given on Wednesday, Saturday and Sunday, and Monday afternoon. The Jeanne Devos museum, in a park, shows a typical old Flemish house with delightful furniture, fire-places and plates – alas, it is only open every second Sunday afternoon from 1 April to 30 October.

The church of St Martin witnessed a miracle on 25 April 1406 when the face of the Virgin changed and tears flowed from her eyes. Not surprisingly, she became a centre for pilgrims.

The main square, lined with lovely chestnut trees, and with a bandstand in the middle still used by the local musicians, is the scene of many fairs, markets and festivals. There is the weekly market on Wednesday morning, the fairs and flea markets of the autumn, and the great carnivals on the last Sunday before Palm Sunday and the first Sunday in July, when the giants Roi des Mitrons and Melanie inspect their town to the music of Wormhout's very own group, the Buckenaeres.

You can learn bowling the Flemish way in the main square using flat discs for bowls, and try real Flemish dishes in the restaurants around. They even have a Windmill Day on the second Sunday in September.

So, if you think Flanders is flat and dull, take the D916 and D933, not the motorways, from Dunkerque to Lille, and see Bergues, Wormhout, Cassel and Bailleul. They are true Flanders.

TOURIST INFORMATION Town hall (28.65.63.72)

MARKETS See above

RESTAURANTS

Belle Vue (28.62.81.81): old Flemish dishes. MEALS C–E. Shut August.

Moulin (28.42.49.96). *Potje vleesch* (chicken, rabbit and veal terrine) and other traditional dishes. MEALS B–E.

M A P S

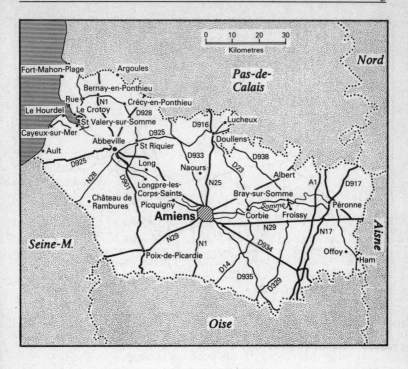

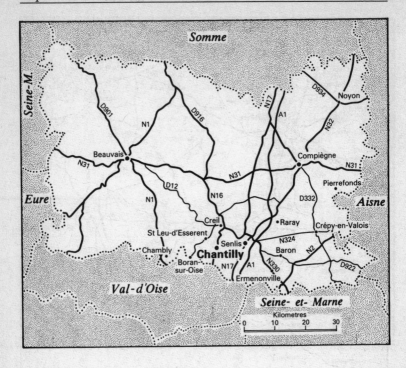

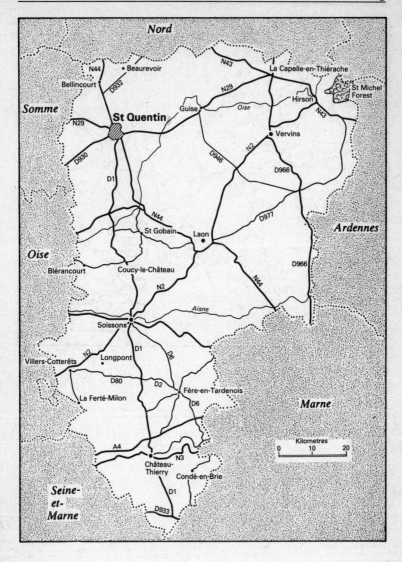

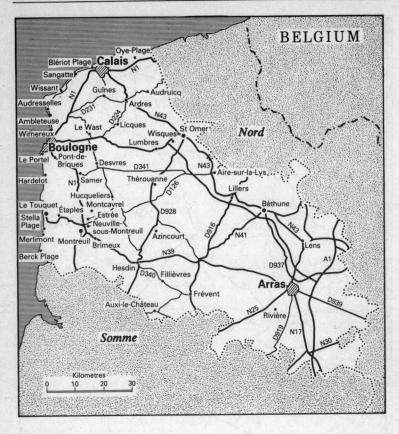

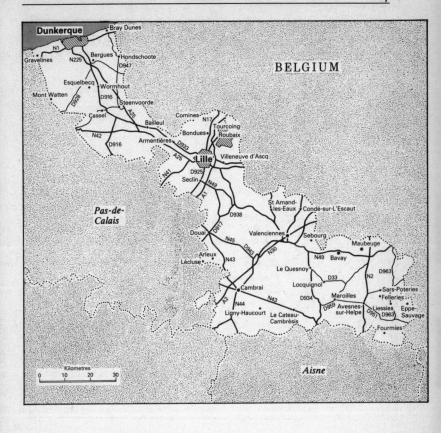

I N D E X

Names of hotels and restaurants appear in *italics*.

All Pan books are available at your local bookshop or newsagent, or can be ordered direct from the publisher. Indicate the number of copies required and fill in the form below.

Send to: **CS Department, Pan Books Ltd., P.O. Box 40, Basingstoke, Hants. RG21 2YT.**

or phone: 0256 469551 (Ansaphone), quoting title, author and Credit Card number.

Please enclose a remittance* to the value of the cover price plus: 60p for the first book plus 30p per copy for each additional book ordered to a maximum charge of £2.40 to cover postage and packing.

*Payment may be made in sterling by UK personal cheque, postal order, sterling draft or international money order, made payable to Pan Books Ltd.

Alternatively by Barclaycard/Access:

Card No.

Signature:

Applicable only in the UK and Republic of Ireland.

While every effort is made to keep prices low, it is sometimes necessary to increase prices at short notice. Pan Books reserve the right to show on covers and charge new retail prices which may differ from those advertised in the text or elsewhere.

NAME AND ADDRESS IN BLOCK LETTERS PLEASE:

....

Name————————————————————————————

Address————————————————————————————

————————————————————————————

————————————————————————————

————————————————————————————

3/87